Language Handbook

Grade 6

Printed in the United States of America

ISBN 0-15-306867-1

10 073 2000

HARCOURT BRACE & COMPANY
ORLANDO · ATLANTA · AUSTIN · BOSTON · SAN FRANCISCO · CHICAGO · DALLAS · NEW YORK ·
TORONTO · LONDON

Contents

USING THE HANDBOOK 8

WRITING

The Writing Process 12
Planning Tips 14
    Understanding Task, Audience, and Purpose (TAP) 14
    Gathering Ideas and Information 15
    Narrowing Your Topic 16
    Organizing Your Writing 18
Writing Tips 22
    Getting Started 22
    Writing an Introduction 23
    Writing a Conclusion 23
Polishing Your Writing 24
    Revising Conferences 24
    Using Computers 25
    Expanding Your Writing 26
    Using Figurative Language 28
    Using Exact Words 28
    Editing Wordy Sentences 28
    Edited Draft Model 29
    Proofreading Tips 30
    Proofread Draft Model 31
    Publishing Your Writing 32
    Final Draft Model 33
Writing Approaches 34
    Collaborative Writing 34
    Shared Writing 35
    Writing to Learn 36
    Writing for Yourself 38
    Writing for Others 38

WRITING FORMS

Writing to Entertain and Express 40
    Story: Realistic Fiction 42

TABLE OF CONTENTS

Story: Historical Fiction 44
Story: Folktale 46
Story: Myth 48
Story: Tall Tale 50
Poems: Rhymed and Unrhymed 51
Play 52

Writing to Describe 54

Descriptive Paragraph 56
Character Sketch 57
Descriptive Essay 58

Writing to Inform 60

Personal Narrative 62
Information Paragraph 64
Information Article...............................65
Directions 66
Comparison and Contrast 67
Cause and Effect 68
Writing for Math and Science 69
News Story: Interview Techniques 70
News Story 71
Research Report Outline..........................72
Research Report: Biography 73
Research Report: Science 74
Research Report: Social Studies 76

Writing to Persuade 78

Persuasive Essay 80
Persuasive Letter 81
Book Review 82
Movie Review....................................83
Speech with Visuals 84

Everyday Writing 86

Journals...88
Writer's Notebook................................90
Messages 91
Friendly Letter 92
Business Letter and Envelope 93
Forms 94
Note Taking.....................................96
Summary..97

Writing for a Test 98

Essay Questions 100
Writing to Prompts 101

GRAMMAR, USAGE, & MECHANICS

GRAMMAR

Sentences..104
   Declarative 106
   Interrogative 106
   Exclamatory, Interjections......................107
   Imperative 108
   Complete Subjects and Complete Predicates 109
   Simple Subjects and Simple Predicates 110
      LOOKING AT LANGUAGE 111
   Compound Subjects and Compound Predicates 112
   Simple and Compound Sentences, Coordinating
      Conjunctions......................................114
   Run-on Sentences, Comma Splices.............115
   Clauses and Phrases................................116
   Independent and Dependent Clauses,
      Subordinating Conjunctions 118
   Complex Sentences................................120
      LOOKING AT LANGUAGE 122

Nouns 123
   Common and Proper Nouns....................124
   Singular and Plural Nouns 126
      LOOKING AT LANGUAGE 127
   Possessive Nouns 128

Pronouns 130
   Subject Pronouns and Object Pronouns 132
   Reflexive Pronouns 133
   Pronoun-Antecedent Agreement 134
   Possessive Pronouns...............................136
      LOOKING AT LANGUAGE 137

Adjectives 138
   Adjectives and Articles............................138
   Proper Adjectives 140
   Demonstrative Adjectives 141
   Comparing with Adjectives 142
   Special Forms of Adjectives 144

Verbs 146
   Action Verbs and Linking Verbs................146
   Main Verbs and Helping Verbs 148

Transitive and Intransitive Verbs/
    Direct and Indirect Objects.................................150
Predicate Nominatives and Predicate Adjectives 152
Present, Past, and Future Tenses.............................154
Perfect Tenses...156
Principal Parts of Regular and Irregular Verbs 158

Adverbs 160
    LOOKING AT LANGUAGE 161
    Comparing with Adverbs 162
    Negatives 163

Prepositions 164
    Object of the Preposition...164
    Prepositional Phrase 165
    Adjective Phrase...166
    Adverb Phrase 167

USAGE
Troublesome Words 168
Standard vs. Nonstandard English 170

MECHANICS
Commas
    Introductory Words, Direct Address 172
    Interrupters, Appositives, Series 173
Punctuating Dialogue and Direct Quotations..........174
Titles 176
Abbreviations 177
Handwriting Chart 178

ADDITIONAL PRACTICE

Sentences 180
Complete and Simple Subjects 182
Complete and Simple Predicates..............................184
Compound Subjects and Predicates 186
Simple and Compound Sentences.............................188
Clauses and Phrases..190
Independent and Dependent Clauses 191
Complex Sentences..192
Nouns 194
Possessive Nouns 196
Pronouns 198
Possessive Pronouns..200
Adjectives and Articles...202
Comparing with Adjectives 204
Action Verbs and Linking Verbs................................206
Main Verbs and Helping Verbs 208
Transitive and Intransitive Verbs/Direct and
    Indirect Objects..210
Predicate Nominatives and Predicate Adjectives 212
Present, Past, and Future Tenses................................214
Perfect Tenses...216
Principal Parts/Irregular Verbs 218
Adverbs...220
Comparing with Adverbs/Negatives.........................222
Prepositions, Objects of the Preposition,
    Prepositional Phrases....................................224
Adjective and Adverb Phrases.................................226
Troublesome Words 228
Commas 230
Punctuating Dialogue and Direct Quotations..............232
Titles...234
Abbreviations 236

STUDY SKILLS

Active Reading Strategies..240
Strategies for Reading Fiction 242
Strategies for Reading Nonfiction 244
Vocabulary Strategies...246
Listening and Speaking Strategies............................248
Researching Information 250
The Library 252

INDEX..254

Using the Handbook

A brand-new book can be intriguing. What lies between the colorful covers? It might be news you can use, points of view you can ponder, or information that adds to your knowledge. Opening a new book is like taking the first step on a voyage of discovery. You have just embarked on that voyage. You may want to skim the pages to see what lies ahead.

WHAT IS A HANDBOOK?

A handbook is, literally, a book that you can carry conveniently in your hand. It serves as a handy reference guide. This particular handbook deals with the English language. A handbook is the same as a manual. The word *manual* actually comes from a root meaning "hand." Just as you might refer to a manual to work on a bicycle, you can refer to this handbook to work on your language.

In this handbook you will find

- ☑ tips for launching into writing assignments
- ☑ examples of writing forms
- ☑ easy-to-understand rules of grammar
- ☑ practice with language

"The question is," said Alice, "whether you can make words mean so many different things."

SECTIONS OF THE HANDBOOK

Your handbook is divided into five sections. The first three sections are about writing; writing forms; and grammar, usage, and mechanics. The fourth section gives you a chance to practice your language skills, and the fifth section explains helpful study strategies.

WRITING

The writing section is based on a multistep writing process. It shows you how to **plan, draft, polish,** and **publish** your writing.

WRITING FORMS

This section contains models of many of the writing forms you will need to use, from letters to stories, from essays to articles. It is organized according to writing purposes—**entertaining and expressing, describing, informing, persuading, everyday writing,** and **writing for a test.**

STUDY SKILLS

This section suggests strategies you can use to **improve** your skills in reading, listening, speaking, and doing research.

GRAMMAR, USAGE, AND MECHANICS

This section contains easy-to-understand information about parts of speech, types of sentences, capitalization, and punctuation. The pages include **rules** and **exercises that check your understanding of those rules.**

ADDITIONAL PRACTICE

In this section you will find exercises in grammar, mechanics, and usage to help you **practice and apply your language skills.**

> "The question is," said Humpty Dumpty, "which is to be master— that's all."
> —Lewis Carroll
>
> Through the Looking Glass

HOW TO FIND INFORMATION IN THE HANDBOOK

Everyone's language could use a little fixing up. This handbook will help you locate and correct those elements of language that you need to repair. If you were fixing your bicycle, you might look in the table of contents or the index of your manual to find the problem you needed to repair. Use the table of contents and index of this handbook the same way.

The **table of contents** begins on page 2. It gives a listing of the main sections of the book with their page numbers. In addition, each section of the book has its own table of contents, as on page 11.

The **index** is in the back of the book. It is useful when you want to find all references to a specific topic. Topics are listed in alphabetical order.

Look for **cross-references** on some pages. They lead you to other pages with related information you might be able to use. An example of a cross-reference appears at the bottom of page 21.

I need help writing a business letter!

Writing

The Writing Process   12

Planning Tips   14

Writing Tips   22

Polishing Your Writing   24

Writing Approaches   34

The Writing Process

Writing can be like taking a journey through your own imagination. You begin with a destination in mind, but the road you take to get there may not be direct. As you travel, you sometimes make discoveries that lead you in new directions. There is no right or wrong road, but the writing process provides a map to guide you.

PREWRITING

Identify your TAP— task, audience, and purpose. Then choose a topic. Gather and organize information about the topic.

DRAFTING

Put your ideas in writing. Don't worry about making mistakes. You can fix them later.

RESPONDING AND REVISING

Reread your writing to see if it fulfills your purpose. Meet with a partner or with a group to discuss it.

As you write, you may choose to exit to another stage in the writing process before continuing. You may choose the same exit more than once. You may pass an exit and return to it later. It's your choice—you, the writer, are in the driver's seat.

There is in writing the constant joy of sudden discovery . . .
—H. L. Mencken

PROOFREADING

Correct spelling, grammar, usage, mechanics, and capitalization errors.

PUBLISHING

Decide how you want to publish your work. Share your writing.

Planning Tips

You may choose your own TAP, or your TAP may be assigned to you.

A blank page can be intimidating. Luckily, writers have discovered many ways to overcome that blank page. Some of their planning tips may help you, too.

> ## UNDERSTANDING TASK, AUDIENCE, AND PURPOSE (TAP)

What kind of writing will I do? Who will read my writing? Why will I write? Every writer faces these questions before putting pencil to paper or fingers to keyboard. The answers to these questions become a writer's **task**, **audience**, and **purpose** (TAP). Once you have defined your TAP, you will find it easier to begin writing.

Task

- **What kind of writing will I do?**

  The answer to what kind of writing you will do might be

  a poem
  a story
  a research report

Audience

- **Who will read my writing?**

  The answer to who will read your writing might be

  a teacher
  a friend
  a committee

Purpose

- **Why am I writing?**

  The answer to why you are writing might be

  to inform
  to explain
  to persuade
  to entertain
  to describe

GATHERING IDEAS AND INFORMATION

Sudden inspiration is great when it comes, but don't count on its coming without some work. Here are some ways to help you find those brilliant ideas:

- **Pick your own brain, and make a list of your ideas for writing.**

- **Brainstorm possible topics with friends. Take notes on their ideas.**

- **Look elsewhere for ideas. Check**

  your journal   *a reference book*
  your portfolio   *magazines*

- **Freewrite—just write everything that comes into your mind, whether it's about your topic or not.**

- **Try a newspaper-writer's trick: Write the words *who*, *what*, *when*, *where*, *why*, and *how*. Then answer each question for your topic.**

When all else fails, incubate— wait a while. The best ideas may take some time to hatch.

PREWRITING STRATEGIES

NARROWING YOUR TOPIC

Once you have decided on your task, audience, and purpose, and you have brainstormed some topics, you may want to spend some time narrowing your topic. It is a rare writer who can simply sit down and roll words onto the page. Try using graphic organizers to help you figure out exactly what you want to write about.

A **web** helps you find related topics when your first idea is too broad or too vague.

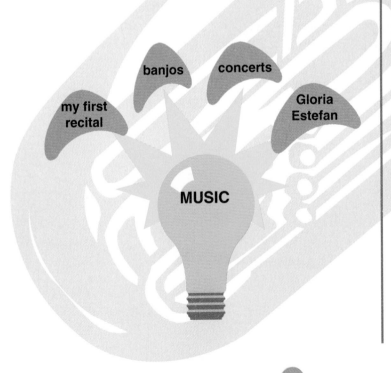

banjos   concerts

my first recital   Gloria Estefan

MUSIC

"My first recital" is a more manageable topic to write about than "music."

Making a **chart** of story elements helps you focus
your thinking.

title: Treasure Cove

setting: The Caribbean;
a tiny, deserted island

characters: Twin sisters, a sea captain

conflict: The sisters hear about a
treasure and hire a devious sea
captain to take them to the island.

An **inverted pyramid** helps you
work from a broad topic to a narrower one.

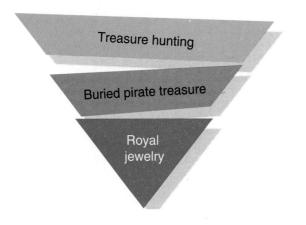

Treasure hunting

Buried pirate treasure

Royal
jewelry

"Treasure hunting" is a
very broad topic.

This is better, but it
would still be a *big*
report.

The inverted pyramid led
to a narrower topic.

ORGANIZING YOUR WRITING

Graphic organizers are useful at more than one point in the writing process. You have seen how to use them to focus on your topic. Now you can use them to help you organize your ideas.

A **cause-effect chart** lets you see at a glance *what happened* and *why*. Sometimes effects become the causes of new effects in a *causal chain*.

More than one kind of graphic organizer may be right for your topic.

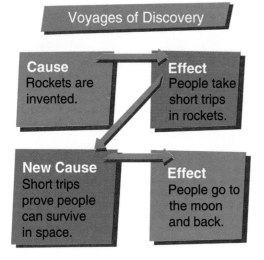

Voyages of Discovery

Cause
Rockets are invented.

Effect
People take short trips in rockets.

New Cause
Short trips prove people can survive in space.

Effect
People go to the moon and back.

18

A **Venn diagram** helps you compare and contrast.

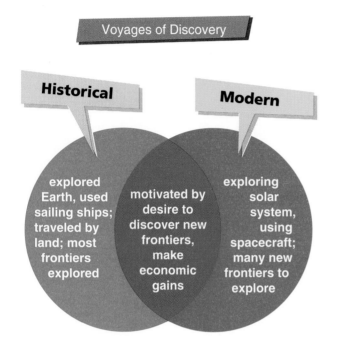

Voyages of Discovery

Historical

Modern

explored Earth, used sailing ships; traveled by land; most frontiers explored

motivated by desire to discover new frontiers, make economic gains

exploring solar system, using spacecraft; many new frontiers to explore

The diagram shows the differences between historical and modern voyages of discovery.

The area of overlap shows how historical and modern voyages of discovery are alike.

A **time line** organizes information in time order.

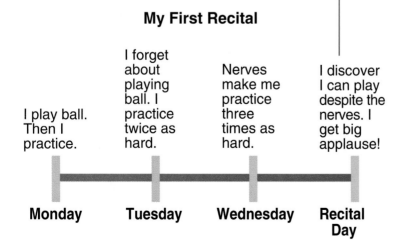

My First Recital

I play ball. Then I practice.

I forget about playing ball. I practice twice as hard.

Nerves make me practice three times as hard.

I discover I can play despite the nerves. I get big applause!

Monday   **Tuesday**   **Wednesday**   **Recital Day**

PREWRITING STRATEGIES

A **how-to chart** organizes steps in time order.

Planning a Recital

Materials

calendar

sheet music

invitations

address book

paper

copy machine

chairs

Steps

1. Set a date.
2. Choose music.
3. Send invitations.
4. Practice!
5. Print programs.
6. Greet and seat guests.
7. Play as well as you can.

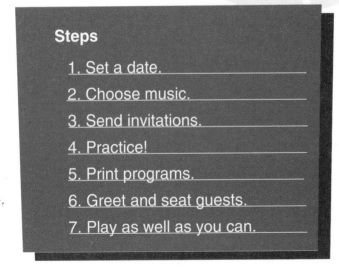

An **outline** can help you organize ideas for fiction or nonfiction.

Treasure Cove

I. **The rising action**
   - A. **Sisters hear about treasure**
   - B. **Hire sea captain to help**

II. **The climax**
   - A. **Sea captain is dishonest**
      1. **Steals map**
      2. **Leaves in lifeboat**
   - B. **Sisters are locked below deck**

III. **The resolution**
   - A. **Sisters escape through porthole**
   - B. **One sister has photographic memory**
      1. **Remembers map**
      2. **Remembers how to sail ship**
   - C. **Sisters beat captain to treasure**

See Research Report Outline, page 72.

Main ideas or major sections are shown with Roman numerals.

Supporting ideas come under them.

Writing Tips

So far you have a topic, ideas, notes, and organizers. You have enough to start writing, *if you choose to write now.* You can always change your mind and start over. You can always take a break, pull over to the side of the road, and think for a while.

GETTING STARTED

If you are ready to write, then *write.* Don't worry yet about how it looks, how it sounds, or whether you put that comma in the right place. Just write. Here are some tips for getting started:

- **Take a deep breath. Relax!**

- **Write as though you are talking to a friend.**

- **Use your imagination. Picture what you are describing. Draw, scribble, sketch!**

- **Start at the end and work backward, or start in the middle and add a beginning and an ending later.**

- **If you can't get started in pencil, switch to pen, crayon, or computer.**

- **Don't forget your planning. Reread your notes, look at your organizers, and remember your TAP.**

WRITING AN INTRODUCTION

An **introduction** is where your reader meets your topic for the first time. A good introduction grabs the reader's imagination and doesn't let it go. It states the main idea and lets the reader know your views. Here are a few ways to make your introduction effective:

- Tell why the reader should care.

- Ask a question that gets the reader thinking.

- Open with a quotation.

WRITING A CONCLUSION

The **conclusion** is the place where everything comes together. It ties up loose ends and summarizes main points.

Here are some tips for writing a good conclusion:

- Restate your main idea in a different, snappy way.

- Review your main points.

- Make a prediction.

Conclusions to avoid:

. . . and then I woke up.

. . . happily ever after.

. . . The End!

Polishing Your Writing

When you **revise**, or edit, your work, you may *add* words, *cut* words, *replace* words, and *move* words. When you polish your writing, you work toward the finished product that pleases you most.

REVISING CONFERENCES

When it comes to polishing writing, nothing is as useful as another pair of eyes. A partner may see problems that you didn't notice or offer new ideas.

Here are some questions to ask yourself or your partner as you revise your work:

- **Does it make sense?**
- **Is the order logical?**
- **Could I add or cut any details?**

Here are some tips for helping other people revise their writing:

- **Tell what you like about it.**
- **Give reasons for your opinions and suggestions.**

Revising is your chance to make your writing say just what you want it to.

USING COMPUTERS

Computers have changed the process of writing. It is now much easier to make changes, polish writing, and save drafts. Computers save time and encourage excellence at every stage of the writing process.

Computers allow you to

- *freewrite* and save your ideas for later
- *add* words simply by inserting them
- *cut* words simply by deleting them
- *replace* words by writing over them
- *move* words, sentences, and paragraphs

Most computers have these handy features:

- a thesaurus, which lets you choose the best word to replace a dull or overused one

  compose *instead of* write

- a spell-checker, which catches mistakes such as this:

  wriet *instead of* write

  but not this:

  right *instead of* write

Of course, a computer's OUTPUT is no better than its INPUT.

RESPONDING AND REVISING STRATEGIES

EXPANDING YOUR WRITING

One way to polish your writing is to *expand* your sentences. Many short, choppy sentences often can be hard to read. Varying the length of your sentences can keep your audience alert and interested.

Combining Sentences

You can expand your writing by joining, or combining, short sentences.

Join two sentences with a comma and a coordinating conjunction such as *and, or,* or *but.*

> *It was July 1. We were going on vacation.*
> *It was July 1, and we were going on vacation.*

Join two closely related sentences with a semicolon.

> *It was July 1; we were going on vacation.*

Join two sentences that share one subject.

> *We saw the Grand Canyon. We visited Yosemite.*
> *We saw the Grand Canyon and visited Yosemite.*

Join two sentences that share one predicate.

> *Dad loved the desert. I loved it, too.*
> *Dad and I loved the desert.*

Editor's Marks

∧	**Add something.**
⅄	**Cut something.**
⟳	**Move something.**
∧	**Replace something.**
/	**Make a lowercase letter.**

Adjectives can tell *which one* or *how many*. They can also describe size, color, kind, and so on. Add adjectives to make sentences vivid.

> *A boulder rose from the plain.*
>
> *A* steel-gray *boulder rose from the* level *plain.*

Adverbs can tell *how, when, where, how often,* or *to what extent.* Add adverbs to give additional information.

> *The burro moved.*
>
> *The burro moved* cautiously.
>
> Finally, *the burro moved.*

Prepositional phrases can act as adjectives or adverbs. Add prepositional phrases to clarify your meaning.

> *Cactuses dotted the landscape.*
>
> *Cactuses* of all sizes *dotted the landscape.*
>
> Across the desert, *cactuses dotted the landscape.*

Examples can help clarify your meaning.

> *Cactuses dotted the landscape.*
>
> *Cactuses*—both prickly pear and saguaro—*dotted the landscape.*

Using Figurative Language

Figurative language, such as similes and metaphors, can add information and clarify meaning in new and creative ways.

- **A simile compares two unlike things using the words *like* or *as.***

  Above, the stars were *as bright as headlights.*

- **A metaphor compares two unlike things without using the words *like* or *as.***

  Above, the stars were *headlights, guiding our steps.*

Using Exact Words

Try to replace ordinary, dull words with vivid words that show your exact meaning. A thesaurus can help you. So can your imagination.

For **pretty,** try *gorgeous, handsome,* or *exquisite.*
For **walk,** try *saunter, stroll,* or *ramble.*
For **dog,** try *poodle, mongrel,* or *collie.*

Editing Wordy Sentences

For livelier writing, cut out unnecessary words.

The huge zucchini squash looked like a ~~big, long,~~ green baseball bat.

Exact words help the reader visualize what you are writing about.

Cut: All baseball bats are *big* and *long,* so these words are not necessary.

A Trip to Blacktop Mesa

The mesa lies just fourty miles west of Pinotchie. It is off the main road. ~~but~~ It is well worth the ~~trip.~~ *detour* Route 230 runs straight *as an arrow* through the desert. *On either side,* The sand is littered with tumble weeds. The landscape is flat *as a pancake*.

Suddenly, Blacktop Mesa rises on the horizon. With walls almost ~~nearly~~ purpendiculer to the flat sand the mesa casts a *huge* shadow across the desert. It is no wonder that the people who first discovered it called it Blacktop. As you come closer, the top *of the mesa* blocks the Sun.

Add: to make the writing less choppy

Replace: to use a more precise noun

Add: to make the description more specific

Add: to give the writing a creative twist

Add: to make the event immediate

Cut: to avoid an unnecessary word

Add: to describe the shadow

Move: to improve the paragraph's logic

Add: to clarify meaning

PROOFREADING TIPS

You have added, cut, moved, and replaced, and your writing is looking more polished. Now is the time to proofread for errors in grammar, usage, spelling, and punctuation. Once you have removed those flaws, your writing will practically glow. Here are some tips for the final polishing stage:

- Reread your writing. Consider reading it aloud.

- Read line by line. Cover up all but the line you're reading, if that helps.

- Circle any words you're unsure of, and check their spelling in a dictionary.

- Look for sentence fragments, run-ons, and comma splices. Add words, cut words, or combine or separate sentences to fix the problem.

- See pages 103–177 for helpful information on grammar, mechanics, and usage.

- Check for neatness. Communication is impossible if your audience can't read your writing.

Proofreader's Marks

≡	Capitalize.
⊙	Add a period.
∧	Add something.
⌃	Add a comma.
⌄⌄	Add quotation marks.
ℛ	Cut something.
⌃	Replace something.
⌒	Close up.
tr	Transpose.
⬭	Spell correctly.
¶	Indent paragraph.
/	Make a lowercase letter.

A Trip to Blacktop Mesa

The mesa lies just ~~fourty~~ *forty* miles west of Pinotchie. It is off the main road, but it is well worth the detour. Route 230 runs straight as an arrow through the desert. On either side, the sand is littered with tumble weeds. The landscape is flat as a pancake.

Suddenly, Blacktop Mesa rises on the horizon. With walls almost ~~purpendiculer~~ *perpendicular* to the flat sand, the mesa casts a huge shadow across the desert. As you come closer, the top of the mesa blocks the sun. It is no wonder that the people who first discovered it called it "Blacktop."

Spell correctly: Check a dictionary if necessary.

Indent paragraph: for logic

Close up: one word

Add a comma: after a long introductory phrase

Make a lowercase letter: to write correctly

Add quotation marks: for correct punctuation

PUBLISHING YOUR WRITING

The word *publish* comes from the same root as the word *public*. To publish your writing is to share it with the public—your audience.

Some writing is private, but most writing is meant to be shared. There are as many ways to publish writing as there are writers. Here are some suggestions. You will think of dozens more.

- Read your writing aloud, or have someone else read it aloud. (You might even record or videotape the reading for future audiences to share.)

- Hand your manuscript or disk to a friend.

- Send a letter through the post office or E-mail.

- Illustrate your writing, and present it as a book, a magazine, a brochure, or a comic book.

- Act it out. (This could work for a journal entry or a story as well as for a play.)

- Display it on a shelf, a bulletin board, or a table.

- Send it to a real-life publisher of books, magazines, or newspapers.

*A word is
dead
When it is
said,
Some say.
I say it just
Begins to
live
That day.
—Emily
Dickinson*

FINAL DRAFT MODEL

Adding, cutting, moving, and replacing words improved this description. Proofreading added the final polish.

A Trip to Blacktop Mesa

You have never seen anything like Blacktop Mesa. The mesa lies just forty miles west of Pinotchie. It is off the main road, but it is well worth the detour.

Route 230 runs straight as an arrow through the desert. On either side, the sand is littered with tumbleweeds. The landscape is flat as a pancake.

Suddenly, Blacktop Mesa rises on the horizon. With walls almost perpendicular to the flat sand, the mesa casts a huge shadow across the desert. As you come closer, the top of the mesa blocks the sun. It is no wonder that the people who first discovered it called it "Blacktop."

This new introduction is more likely to make a reader want to read the description.

Writing Approaches

You probably write often. You write

notes to friends   *test papers*
     to-do lists   *phone messages*

No single approach works for all writing. You may use different approaches at different times.

COLLABORATIVE WRITING

When you **collaborate**, you work with someone else toward a common goal. Sometimes you write with other people—perhaps on a project or a play. Here are some hints to help you write with a group:

- Share ideas. Open your mind to new opinions.

- Share tasks. Each person in your group should have a role to play in getting the job done. For example, the Recorder might record ideas, and the Reader might read information aloud.

- Think about what you do best. How can your talents help your group reach its goal?

- Stay on task. Do not allow the discussion to fall apart. Make sure everyone remembers the group's goal and works toward it.

Reasons to write with a group:
- *Many hands make light work.*
- *Two heads are better than one.*

SHARED WRITING

Shared writing is writing you do with a partner, usually a teacher or family member. Shared writing frees your imagination. You can talk through your ideas while someone else writes them down.

These suggestions might help a partner you work with, or you might use them when you are a partner for a younger writer.

- **Guide the writer toward a reasonable topic. Ask**

  What is your assignment?
  Do you know enough about the topic?
  Who might want to read about the topic?

- **Guide the writer away from bad choices. Ask**

  How might this be made clearer?
  Is this word the best one to use here?
  Should you add or cut any information?

- **Guide the writer toward a chosen goal. Ask**

  How do you feel about the finished work?
  Does this say all you want to say?
  Does it fulfill the assignment?

A good partner is a guide, not a boss.

35

WRITING TO LEARN

Writing to learn is writing that helps you organize or absorb knowledge. Here are some examples:

- **Comparing**   While shopping for a bike, you jot down impressions of the ones you look at.

- **Summarizing**   You keep track of the movies you see by writing brief paragraphs that include their stars and plots.

- **Observing**   During Nature Club, you take notes on the bird calls you hear in the woods.

- **Classifying**   To organize your homework, you write the assignments in subject-area categories on a chart.

Good Opportunities for Writing to Learn

- **Before a discussion, write some questions.**

- **After a discussion, jot down your thoughts.**

- **While studying, take notes.**

- **After studying, review your knowledge.**

- **After an assignment, tell what you learned.**

- **Before a lengthy writing task, write some short sketches that you might include in the longer piece.**

You can use writing to learn to think through any kind of content reading you may do in such areas as science or social studies. On the left side of your notebook page, take notes on your reading. On the right, jot down questions or your own interpretations.

Writing to learn is often private or unshared.

Landforms

mountains
hills   What makes a mountain
plains   different from a hill?
plateaus
                         Where are these?

Regions of U.S.

Pacific coast
intermountain   (like Arizona and Utah)
Rockies
interior plains   Great Plains, etc.
Appalachians   (including us in VT!)
Canadian shield
                         not too important
coastal plains

WRITING FOR YOURSELF

One way or another, all the writing you do is for yourself. When you write, you take a trip through your imagination, learning new things about yourself along the way.

Some writing is truly private. Your diary is not meant to be shared. Grocery lists; to-do lists; lists of dreams, plans, and ideas—all of these are just for you. You have great freedom when you write for yourself. You can even use your own shorthand:

I   P J   Buy 2 ts.

You polish this writing only if *you* want to.

WRITING FOR OTHERS

Writing for others implies a certain responsibility. Your goal is to *communicate*—to make yourself understood. That means you must use certain standards of grammar and punctuation. You must choose the best possible words to get your point across. Remember that you have a passenger—your reader—with you on your journey. You will never see exactly the same things along the route, but putting forth your best effort will ensure that your passenger enjoys the ride.

Writing Forms

Writing to Entertain and Express   40

Writing to Describe   54

Writing to Inform   60

Writing to Persuade   78

Everyday Writing   86

Writing for a Test   98

Writing to Entertain and Express

You should always write with a purpose in mind. Sometimes your purpose is to **entertain**—to amuse, touch, or thrill your reader. Sometimes you write to **express** your own feelings and thoughts. When your purpose is to entertain or express, you may want to think about these things as you go through the steps of the writing process.

PREWRITING

Choosing a Topic

- **What from my own experience might amuse, move, or thrill a reader?**

- **What kinds of stories do I like to read?**

- **Did anything happen recently that affected me deeply?**

- **Would this topic work best as a story, a poem, or a play?**

Gathering Information

- **What setting should I use?**

- **Who are the main characters?**

- **What ideas from my journal can I use?**

- **Would a list of vivid words help me focus my writing?**

DRAFTING

- Would using dialogue or description help me let my audience hear and see what I am telling about?

- Do I have a beginning, a middle, and an ending?

RESPONDING AND REVISING

- Does the order of events I describe make sense?

- Have I used words that are vivid and clear?

- Can I add details to help my audience understand?

PROOFREADING

- Have I capitalized the title properly?

- Did I punctuate dialogue correctly?

PUBLISHING

- Could illustrations add interest to what I have written?

- How can I share my work with the audience I have chosen?

EXPRESSIVE WRITING MODELS

Realistic Fiction,
pages 42–43

Historical Fiction,
pages 44–45

Folktale,
pages 46–47

Myth,
pages 48–49

Tall Tale,
page 50

Rhymed and Unrhymed Poems,
page 51

Play,
pages 52–53

MODEL: REALISTIC FICTION

Realistic fiction *tells a story that could be true but is not. It features characters and settings that are based on the real world.*

Michael Jordan for a Day

introduces the main
character and the
problem

Leon had always been short, even as a baby. This would not have been so bad, but Leon wanted to play basketball, and basketball players are tall. After all, the whole point of basketball is to toss a ball through a hoop several miles above the ground.

use of humor
to add interest

Leon tried out for the team anyway. He dribbled and passed well and even made a basket or two.

sentences of different
lengths for variety

"Here's my Michael Jordan shot," said Leon. The ball whipped through the net.

Then the coach sent in Rick "The Stick" Walters to guard Leon. Rick Walters was named "The Stick" for a reason. He was thin and very, very tall. Poor Leon could not get past him and could not shoot over him.

"Your Michael Jordan shot does you a lot of good now," sneered Stick.

"You're a good ball handler, Leon," said the coach. "I'll let you practice with the team, but I have to tell you the truth: Don't expect to play."

Leon practiced all season with the team. He worked hard. Even Stick was impressed.

During every game, Leon sat on the bench cheering. How he wanted to play! Toward the end of the season, one of the regular players was injured. Finally Leon got his chance. Stick was ready when the coach sent Leon in.

"I'll block Leon's guy and my own guy," said Stick. "Go, Leon."

Leon did not have time to be surprised. He nabbed the ball and dribbled madly. No one could get to Leon because of Stick.

"Here's my Michael Jordan shot," he whispered. The ball whipped through the net. With Stick's help, Leon had won the game!

dialogue to move the action along

story told in time order

ending that satisfies readers

NARRATIVE WRITING

MODEL: HISTORICAL FICTION

Historical fiction *is realistic fiction that takes place at a specific time in the past. Historical fiction relies on details of time and place to paint a picture of an earlier world.*

Alicia Troy, Minutegirl

setting

The year was 1775. All over Massachusetts, men were forming militias for the fight they feared would come. Benjamin Troy and his son Daniel joined the Minutemen in their town, Lexington. Every few days, they were called to drill. As the women of the town gathered in the square, they often saw the men marching up the main street.

cultural details from a specific time and place

Alicia Troy watched this with growing excitement. She was never content to sit home by the fire, darning her brother's socks or embroidering her sampler. She wished that she could drill with her father and brother.

accurate historical details

One evening Alicia was left at home as the men went off to drill. As she sat glumly by the window spinning wool, she saw something frightening. A column of men in red coats was marching up the long road toward Lexington.

dialogue to move the
story forward

If these British soldiers saw the Minutemen drilling, there might be trouble.

Alicia ran out the back door and saddled her horse. She rode through the woods until she reached the clearing where the Minutemen drilled. She jumped off her horse and marched up to Colonel Adams.

"Colonel, there is a column of redcoats perhaps ten minutes away," said Alicia.

The colonel disbanded his troops, and they scattered in all directions.

"Alicia Troy, you have done well," said the colonel. "You are a good spy and a clever girl. I will name you an honorary Minuteman."

"Thank you, Colonel," Alicia said, "but I would rather be called a Minutegirl."

The colonel laughed, touched his hat, and rode off. Benjamin and Daniel hugged Alicia, and they rode home together.

See Punctuating Dialogue and Direct Quotations, pages 174–175.

MODEL: FOLKTALE

Traditionally, a **folktale** is a story handed down from generation to generation. Folktales sometimes feature fantastic events and may teach a lesson. Some explain the origins of something in nature. Modern folktales include the same elements.

Friends Forever

time and place clearly indicated

Long, long ago, meadows filled the lands between the mountains. The meadows were full of flowers of every color. Some of the most beautiful were striped with orange and black.

fantastic events

In those days, the flowers could talk to one another and to all the passing breezes. Some of the breezes had traveled all the way to the sea. The orange-and-black flowers were spellbound by their stories of crashing waves and velvety fog.

problem introduced

"I wish I could see the ocean," one sighed. "It must be the most marvelous thing in the world."

"No, it isn't," said a small blue flower softly.

dialogue to move action along

"The most wonderful thing is to be right here in the meadow. I love to wake up in the spring and watch the year change."

Just then a magic breeze brushed by. "I've

been listening to you," it said. "Do you really want to see the ocean?"

"Oh, yes," cried the orange-and-black flower.

"Then you shall have your wish," said the magic breeze.

problem solved

The orange-and-black flower felt a gentle tug. Suddenly it was flying! It had been turned into a butterfly.

"Good-bye," called the blue flower.

"Good-bye," said the butterfly. "I'll be back to see you next year."

natural occurrence explained

And the butterfly kept its promise. Every year the orange-and-black monarch butterflies visit their old friends in the meadows and tell them stories of the sea. But the other flowers are content to stay in the meadows and watch the seasons come and go.

Lesson: Friends can like different things.

MODEL: MYTH

Myths usually explain natural events. They may tell the story of gods and goddesses or humans, and they often involve supernatural acts.

The Pine Cone

At one time, the seeds of the pine tree were quite exposed. They were bright and shiny, and they were extremely attractive to birds and squirrels.

problem

Alas, this meant that the seeds were eaten instead of dropping to the ground to develop into new pine trees. All over the land, pine trees were becoming scarce.

At last, the chief goddess announced a contest. She would give a prize to the god or goddess who devised the best plan to protect the pine tree's seeds.

Soon the gods met to share their ideas. The chief goddess called each one forward.

The god of secrets had designed a shining silver case for the pine seeds.

"I'm afraid this won't work. It will just make the seeds even more attractive to magpies and squirrels," said the chief goddess.

The goddess of the hunt had made a coating of prickly golden arrows for the pine seeds.

dialogue to move the
story forward

supernatural explanation
for natural occurrence

"This is good," said the chief goddess, "but it is too colorful. We may use this design for a meadow plant instead of for a tree."

The god of war had made armor for the pine seeds, using a material that looked like wood.

"Here is the winner," said the chief goddess. "This design not only protects the seeds but camouflages them as well."

Since that time, pine tree seeds have been enclosed in a woody armor. Pine trees are again found all over the land.

See Punctuating Dialogue and Direct Quotations, pages 174–175.

MODEL: TALL TALE

*A **tall tale** uses exaggeration and humor to tell a story. Its characters and their problems are larger than life.*

The Floods of '25

informal, chatty tone

Did you ever hear what caused the great floods of '25? Well, way up the river, right about where it starts, twin boys lived with their mom. One twin was as large as the other, and

vivid language to spark interest

each was as large as a Douglas fir. In the spring of '25, Mom needed water for her

exaggeration for humorous effect

garden, so one twin started digging a well. Pretty soon, he'd dug to the center of the earth. He had worked up a little sweat digging, so the other twin jumped in and took over.

It didn't take long for the twins to work their way through the earth to the other side. They came up in a huge lake. The twins went back home and drew water through straws.

silly explanation for real-life event

Pretty soon, Mom's garden had washed clear away, along with most of the Atchoo Valley. Now you know: It was Mom's well that caused the floods of '25.

MODEL: RHYMED POEM

a pattern of rhythm and rhyme

Poetry can express a mood or paint a picture with just a few words. Poetry is usually written in rhythmic lines rather than in sentences. In a rhymed poem, syllable sounds are repeated at the ends of paired lines. For example, the following poem follows a rhyme scheme, or pattern, of a/b/a/b: the first and third lines rhyme, and the second and fourth lines rhyme.

A sleeping fawn,
A single crow—
Above, the dawn.
Still night below.

MODEL: UNRHYMED POEM

imagery strengthened by rhythm

In unrhymed poetry, rhythm, figurative language, and imagery express a mood.

The quiet night
Gentle breathing of branches.
The sun creeps
Glinting edges of hilltops.
A crow calls
Shrill salute to the morning.

See Using Figurative Language and Using Exact Words, page 28.

MODEL: PLAY

*A **play** tells a story through dialogue. Plays are meant to be acted out. Stage directions in parentheses indicate action and emotions, and dialogue moves the play forward.*

Mr. Anderson's Magic Pepper

cast of characters

MR. ANDERSON, a shopkeeper
MAY, his granddaughter
SAM, his grandson
DONNA, May's friend

setting

(The play takes place inside MR. ANDERSON'S shop.)

capital letters for speakers' names

MR. ANDERSON: May, what's wrong?

dialogue (without quotation marks)

MAY: (sobbing) Oh, Grandpa, that mean old Sam was making fun of me again. He picks on me all the time!

DONNA: Mr. Anderson, Sam is really mean. He always makes May cry.

MAY: It's just little things that he does, but they make me feel bad.

MR. ANDERSON: Well, we will see about that. Tell Sam I have something special for him in my shop.

DONNA: Mr. Anderson, what are you planning?

MR. ANDERSON: Just find Sam. I will take care of him. I will cure him of his unkind ways.

stage directions to show action	(The girls exit. MR. ANDERSON picks up a pepper plant.)
	(MAY and DONNA enter, followed by SAM.)
	SAM: What've you got for me, Grandpa?
stage directions to show emotions	MR. ANDERSON: (calmly) This, Sam. It's a special pepper that will cure you.
	SAM: Cure me? I'm not sick! Let's see it!
	(MR. ANDERSON picks a small pepper and hands it to SAM.)
story moves along through dialogue	SAM: Big deal! A pepper. Who cares?
	MR. ANDERSON: Not just a pepper—a very small pepper. It is just right for a big guy like you. Taste it!
	(SAM bites the pepper, and tears begin to pour down his cheeks.)
	SAM: It's hot! Waaaaaaah!
	MAY: (astonished) Sam's crying!
satisfying conclusion	MR. ANDERSON: Now he knows what it feels like when little things make you cry. Perhaps this ordinary little pepper will cure you, Sam, of causing tears in others.

See Adverbs, page 160.

Writing to Describe

When you write to describe, you try to let your audience share your particular vision. Precise words are a vital part of descriptive writing. Here are some things to think about when you are writing a description:

PREWRITING

Choosing a Topic

- What have I seen or heard that a reader might appreciate?

- Do I know someone who is interesting or special?

- Is this subject appropriate for a short description?

Gathering Information

- What adjectives describe this subject?

- If the subject is a person, how does that person walk, eat, and talk?

- Can I get additional ideas for details to include from a magazine or a photography book?

- Could I use freewriting—writing down everything I picture about my subject?

DRAFTING

- How will I introduce my topic?
- In what order will I describe this topic? Top to bottom? Left to right?

RESPONDING AND REVISING

- Are all my details essential to the description?
- Could I replace any words with more precise ones?
- Have I made the topic come alive? Will my readers get a clear picture?

PROOFREADING

- Have I used commas in a series correctly?
- Did I misspell any words?

PUBLISHING

- Should I illustrate my work or let the words paint the picture?
- Can I make this into a brochure or a poster?

DESCRIPTIVE WRITING MODELS

Descriptive Paragraph, page 56

Character Sketch, page 57

Descriptive Essay, pages 58–59

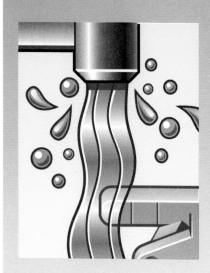

Writing to Describe

MODEL: DESCRIPTIVE PARAGRAPH

A **descriptive paragraph** appeals to the reader's senses of sight, hearing, smell, touch, and taste. In a few words, it paints a picture of a subject.

topic sentence

vivid verbs

sensory details

Big Lake is prettiest just before sunset. The waves lap gently on the shoreline, and loons call eerily across the water. A breeze carries the spicy scent of pine trees. The sky fades at the edges, turning first light blue, then lilac, then pink, and then orange. Streaky clouds are reflected on the lake. Bass and pickerel dance just below the shimmering surface, sometimes rising up to capture a mosquito. Everything is calm.

See Using Exact Words, page 28, and Action Verbs and Linking Verbs, pages 146–147.

DESCRIPTIVE WRITING

*In a **character sketch**, a single person is described. The writer might tell how the character looks, sounds, and acts. The writer may explain or give opinions about the character by showing other people's reactions. The object is to create an engaging portrait in a few words.*

topic sentence

Carla Washington rarely stood still as a child. She was always on the move in school. Today, Ms. Washington is the busy, successful, inspiring leader everyone predicted she would be. She is also the principal of our school.

character reflected through eyes of others

Ms. Washington strides into the school with a smile for everyone in her path. She knows every one of her students by name, and she makes each one feel special. No matter how busy she is, she always takes the time to listen. No wonder her students voted her Educator of the Year.

interesting details make character come alive

When the last bell rings, most of us show signs of a long and hectic day. Ms. Washington, however, looks as fresh as when the day began. Her curly black hair is perfectly combed, her jacket is as straight as her spine, and she is still smiling. How does she do it?

See Adding Details and Examples, page 27, and Adjectives, pages 138–145.

57

DESCRIPTIVE WRITING

MODEL: DESCRIPTIVE ESSAY

*A **descriptive essay** is longer and more complete than a descriptive paragraph. Like a descriptive paragraph, however, it uses sensory details to paint a picture.*

Morning in Barbados

introduction

When I am visiting my grandmother and aunt in Barbados, I find that I get up very early. I want to spend every possible moment outdoors. That is because mornings in Barbados are not like mornings anywhere else.

sensory details in time order

Morning in Barbados begins with the crow of a dozen roosters. Moments later, the clop-clop of hooves tells me that our neighbor is leaving for work. Wagon wheels whir and crunch over the rocky dirt road outside.

figurative language

vivid verbs

sensory details in
space order, moving
from east to west

I run to the doorway and look out. To the east, the sun is a ball of fire over the ocean. The waves glisten as though they were brand-new today. Seagulls wheel on the air currents over the cliffs.

Above my grandmother's house, a tree drips dew onto the tin roof. Fat chickens scurry through the yard, pecking at the grass and clucking at each other. I hear Grandmother stir and sigh.

To the west, the road disappears in a sugarcane field. The tall cane shines as the sun hits it. Soon the cane cutters will be working in the field, but now it stands silently, waiting. I stand silently, too, eagerly waiting for another Barbados day to begin.

See Using Figurative Language, page 28, and Action Verbs and Linking Verbs, pages 146–147.

Writing to Inform

Encyclopedia articles, scientific studies, and newspaper stories have one thing in common: They all are written to inform an audience. Sometimes informative writing is meant to instruct or teach. Sometimes it simply relates interesting facts or details. Thinking about these questions will help you if the purpose of your writing is to inform:

PREWRITING

Choosing a Topic

- Am I an expert on any particular topic?
- Is there a topic I would like to know more about?
- Can I find enough material about this topic to write an interesting essay or report?

Gathering Information

- What reference books might help me?
- Can I get information in my journal, from an interview, or in the library?
- Would an outline help me organize my ideas?

DRAFTING

- What do I want my audience to learn?

- Is there a particular order for the information that would be most logical?

RESPONDING AND REVISING

- Will readers understand the important facts?

- Could I write a better conclusion?

- Is there any information I should add?

PROOFREADING

- Did I spell technical terms correctly?

- Have I capitalized all proper nouns?

PUBLISHING

- Could diagrams or illustrations clarify this information?

- How can I share this information with the audience I wish to reach?

INFORMATIVE WRITING MODELS

Personal Narrative, pages 62–63

Information Paragraph, page 64

Information Article, page 65

Directions, page 66

Comparison and Contrast, page 67

Cause and Effect, page 68

Writing for Math and Science, page 69

News Story, pages 70–71

Research Report Outline, page 72

Biography, page 73

Science, pages 74–75

Social Studies, pages 76–77

MODEL: PERSONAL NARRATIVE

*In a **personal narrative**, the writer tells about a personal experience. A personal narrative is autobiographical, but it typically focuses on a specific event.*

Playing for Fun

interesting opening

I have always been miserable at sports. I cannot see balls when they fly at my head, and I always end up injuring myself or someone else. Once, I even managed all by myself to cause my softball team to lose the championship game in the ninth inning. It was not until our class picnic that I learned that even I can succeed at sports.

mix of sentence types

I was not even going to play in the volleyball game. After all, who would want me to play? The teams were uneven, however, and my friend Paul yelled at me to join. I was sure that everyone on the field was groaning inside, but they acted friendly as I stood stupidly in the back row.

details in time order

A few volleys later, I realized something strange. No one was keeping score! I asked what the score was, and someone said, "Who knows? We're just playing for fun."

direct appeal to audience

We're just playing for fun? What a strange concept that was! If there were no score, then my clumsy efforts would not count. Suddenly I felt free to run for the ball. I even managed to hit it over the net—several times!

After the game, we all lay on the grass, exhausted. To the beat of my pounding heart, I kept thinking, "I wasn't bad. I wasn't bad." If you are any kind of athlete, you cannot imagine how difficult this was for me to accept. After all, I had been the worst athlete at whatever game I played for as long as I could remember.

ending that both summarizes and expands

I am beginning to think that some people are just not meant to compete. These days, when I am in a competitive situation, I just pretend there is no score, grade, or judgment involved. When I simply "play for fun," everything comes easily to me.

See Writing an Introduction and Writing a Conclusion, page 23, and Combining Sentences, page 26.

MODEL: INFORMATION PARAGRAPH

*An **information paragraph** gives condensed information about a specific topic.*

topic sentence

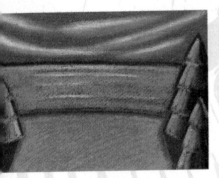

supporting details

The United States contains several of the largest lakes in the world. Three of the Great Lakes are among the world's top ten lakes in square mileage. Lake Superior is the largest lake in this country, with an area of 31,800 square miles. Lakes Huron and Michigan have areas of 23,000 and 22,400 square miles, respectively. If you put all five Great Lakes together with their connecting waterways, they form the largest body of fresh water anywhere in the world.

See Adding Details and Examples, page 27, and Common and Proper Nouns, pages 124–125.

*An **information article** gives details on a specific topic. It generally contains three or more paragraphs.*

The Spingarn Medal

introduction

The Spingarn Medal is awarded each year by the NAACP for the highest achievement by an African American. It has been awarded to famous people and to little-known people who have made a difference.

details and examples

Entertainers and athletes who have won the award include singer Lena Horne and baseball great Hank Aaron. In 1956 the medal went to Dr. Martin Luther King, Jr. The very next year, it was awarded to a group—Daisy Bates and the Little Rock Nine. Ms. Bates was president of the NAACP in Arkansas. In 1957 she and nine high school students were responsible for integrating a high school in Little Rock, Arkansas.

conclusion

Reading the list of winners of the Spingarn Medal is like reading a history of African Americans in the twentieth century. From Leontyne Price to Ralph Bunche, these are people who have made a difference. This award honors their outstanding contributions.

See Writing an Introduction and Writing a Conclusion, page 23, and Adding Details and Examples, page 27.

MODEL: DIRECTIONS

Directions *may tell how to do something, how to make something, or how to get somewhere. They must be written in a logical order so that they can be followed easily.*

topic sentence

materials needed

time-order words to show logical sequence

Baba ghanouj is my favorite sandwich spread or dip, and it is easy to make. You need several small eggplants, lemon juice, tahini (sesame-seed paste), garlic, and scallions. First, wash the eggplants and pierce them with a fork. Next, bake them on a cookie sheet at 400°F. for one hour. While they cool, chop three garlic cloves. When the eggplants are cool enough to touch, scoop their insides into a bowl. Stir in the garlic, six tablespoons of lemon juice, and four tablespoons of tahini. Mash everything together with a fork. Finally, chop a scallion or two and sprinkle on top. Your baba ghanouj is ready to eat.

See Adverbs, page 160.

MODEL: COMPARISON AND CONTRAST

*A **comparison** shows how two subjects are alike. A **contrast** shows how they differ. Sometimes comparison and contrast are used in a single piece of writing.*

topic sentence

points of comparison

topic sentence

points of contrast

Because they have a lot in common, bald eagles and ospreys are often mistaken for each other. Both are extremely large birds of prey. They often live in the same territory, and you may see either one soaring gracefully above the earth. Both hunt mostly fish.

If you know what to look for, however, you can tell these birds apart. Seen from below, the bald eagle is mostly dark, while the osprey is mostly light. The bald eagle soars with flat wings, but the osprey has a crook in its wings. Bald eagles prefer their fish dead or on the verge of dying. Ospreys, on the other hand, are the only large birds of prey that dive feet first into the water after live fish.

See Combining Sentences, page 26, and Adding Details and Examples, page 27.

MODEL: CAUSE AND EFFECT

*In **cause-and-effect writing,** the writer tells about a cause that produces certain effects. The writer could also tell about certain effects and trace them back to their cause. Cause-and-effect writing can begin with either the cause or the effect.*

topic sentence to be discussed

Survival in the harsh environment of a desert is not easy. The bright sunlight, intense heat, and lack of water produce varied adaptations in the local plant life and animals.

examples

For example, desert plants grow far apart because there is so little water. Some plants, such as the mesquite tree, have very deep roots to locate water far below. Other plants, including the barrel cactus, store water in their large trunks.

topic sentence that shifts the focus

Animals that live in the desert have made many unusual adaptations to survive the difficult conditions.

additional examples

Most desert animals look for food at night to avoid the intense daylight heat. Small animals, such as snakes and rodents, burrow underground to stay cool. Large animals try to stay in the shade. Some desert animals, like the famous camel, actually store fat, which they can convert into water. That is the function of the humps on the camel's back.

Writing about math *may take the form of directions or information. Specialized words should be explained and used correctly.*

topic sentence

steps in order

solution

It is easy to find the width of a rectangle when you know its length and area. In a rectangle, opposite sides have the same measurement. Call the width w and the length l. The area of a rectangle (A) equals the width times the length, or (w) x (l). Therefore, the area divided by l equals w, the width.

Science writing *may be in the form of lab reports, articles, or research reports. Writers must keep their audience in mind and adequately explain any technical terms.*

topic sentence

method

results

On September 25, our team studied the plant life in a marked area. We marked off a 1-meter square and divided it into fourths. Each of us sampled the plant life in one-fourth of the area.

Ninety percent of the plant life was bluegrass. The next most common plant was red clover. We found one dandelion, two chicory plants, two teasels, and an unidentified grasslike plant.

See Writing to Learn, page 36.

NEWS STORY: INTERVIEW TECHNIQUES

A **news story** provides current factual information and answers these questions: who, what, when, where, and sometimes why and how. The information often comes from a living source—a person. Here are some interview techniques that can help you gather information:

- At the top of a sheet of paper, write the subject's name and facts you already know about the person.

- Before the interview, write a list of questions to ask.

- At the interview, write down the answers. If you want to use a tape recorder, ask permission first.

- Depending on the answers you get, change the questions or their order.

- Be polite, listen carefully, and say thank you.

Maria Sanchez, candidate for president of the school board

1. *Tell me a bit about yourself.*
2. *Why did you decide to run for office?*
3. *How did you first get involved with the school board?*
4. *What issues does the school board face?*
5. *When do you think changes can be made?*

EXPOSITORY/NARRATIVE WRITING

A news story contains a headline, *a* lead, *and a* body. *It gives information about a current event, an issue, or a person.*

headline

Sanchez Seeks Presidency of School Board

lead telling *who, what, where, when,* **and** *why*

Maria Sanchez, a local business executive, is running for president of the school board in Duane County this year because she wants to make the board more responsive to the needs of students and their taxpaying parents.

body telling *how*

Sanchez, who grew up in Duane County and attended its public schools, says she wants to help students realize their full potential. She wants the board to focus on keeping potential dropouts in school and on spending tax dollars where they can do the most good.

"Head Start and Students in Business are examples of two successful programs I would continue to support," Sanchez says. "Let's fund programs that work."

Sanchez would like to change the way board meetings are run. If elected, she would encourage students to participate as nonvoting members of the board. Sanchez believes she can accomplish most of these changes within the first six months if she is elected.

See Interview Techniques, page 70, and Punctuating Dialogue and Direct Quotations, pages 174–175.

MODEL: RESEARCH REPORT OUTLINE

Lengthy informative writing, such as a **research report,** may be organized by using an outline. An outline uses Roman numerals for main topics, capital letters for subtopics, and Arabic numerals for details.

Jacob Riis

main topics

I. Early life
A. Born in Denmark in 1849
B. Moved to New York City

II. Reform work

never an A without a B;

A. Police reporter
1. Firsthand look at poverty
2. Firsthand look at crime

never a 1 without a 2

B. Crusader supported by Theodore Roosevelt
1. An improved water supply
2. Changes in child labor laws
3. Renovation of slums

III. Major works
A. How the Other Half Lives (1890)
B. The Making of an American (1901)
1. Autobiography
2. Description of his crusades

See Organizing Your Writing, pages 18–21.

*A **biography** tells the story of a real person. A biography is usually presented in time order and includes interesting facts about the person.*

title

Jacob Riis, Crusader

introduction

Jacob Riis was born in Denmark in 1849, but New York City claims him as a native son. Jacob Riis grew up to become a crusader for the rights of the poor. He was one of the most important reformers of the muckraking era.

details in time order

Riis worked for more than twenty years as a police reporter. This job gave him a firsthand look at poverty and crime. He wrote about what he saw, and soon his work caught the attention of Theodore Roosevelt. This led to an improved water supply, changes in the child labor laws, and the renovation of some terrible slums.

Riis's major works are <u>How the Other Half Lives</u>, published in 1890, and <u>The Making of an American</u>, published in 1901. <u>The Making of an American</u> is autobiographical. It tells of Riis's love of America and of his crusade to help our country fulfill its promise of opportunity for everyone.

See Writing an Introduction and Writing a Conclusion, page 23, and Titles, page 176.

MODEL: RESEARCH REPORT—SCIENCE

A science report relies on facts and information from several sources. The writer usually attempts to answer a question.

How Snakes Slither

Long ago, people believed that snakes walked on their ribs. They thought that the ribs acted as if they were several pairs of legs. We know now that this is not true. How then do snakes slither?

Along a snake's belly lie rows of overlapping scutes, or scales. Each scute is attached by muscles to a pair of the snake's ribs. When a scute is pulled back by the muscles, its edge pushes against the ground. When the scute is pushed forward by the muscles, it slides over the ground.

A snake moves the overlapping scutes on its belly in groups. With each movement, some scutes push against the ground, and others slide forward. This allows the snake to move forward in a straight line.

In another common method of movement, the snake flexes its muscles to produce a series of waves down the length of its body. The curves of the body push against the ground, moving the snake forward.

a topic that is not too broad

specialized words defined and explained

A few desert snakes use a strange form of movement called sidewinding. The snake arches the front of its body upward and throws its head to one side. It then pulls its body across and throws its head to the other side. Because sand gives the snake little to push against, sidewinding works better than other forms of movement would.

Describing in detail the way snakes move makes their movements sound jerky. In fact, their movements are very smooth and efficient. Undulating muscles and overlapping scutes move snakes forward steadily at an average speed of about two miles per hour.

See Organizing Your Writing, pages 18–21, and Writing for Math and Science, page 69.

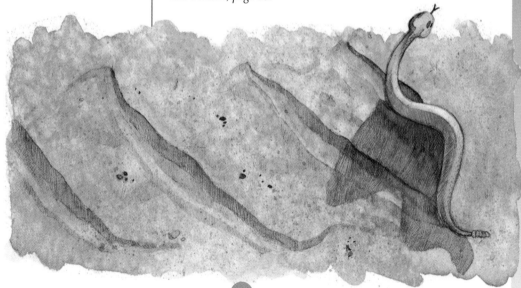

MODEL: RESEARCH REPORT— SOCIAL STUDIES

*A **social studies report** may give information about a single topic, or it may compare and contrast more than one topic. As with any research report, the writer uses a variety of sources to gather information.*

title

Voting Rights—The Road to Equality

introduction

Throughout most of American history, women did not enjoy the same rights as men. They could not own land. They could not make decisions about how their children were to be educated. Most importantly, they could not vote.

details in time order

In the 1820s and 1830s, a number of white women began protesting the inequalities of slavery. It was through this struggle for human rights that they began to see the more subtle inequalities in their own lives.

In 1848 a number of important women activists, including Elizabeth Cady Stanton and Lucretia Mott, organized a woman suffrage convention at Seneca Falls, New York.

The delegates to the convention issued a proclamation based on the Declaration of Independence. In the

quotations from

another source

document they said that "all men and women are created equal." They demanded that women be given "all the

details in time order

rights and privileges which belong to them as citizens of the United States."

Winning these rights took longer than expected. During the 1890s, several of the new western states gave women the right to vote. Eventually, some of the eastern and midwestern states did likewise. However, women still could not vote in national elections. That right was finally won in 1920 when the Nineteenth Amendment to the Constitution was ratified. At last, the right to have a say in the way the country is governed applied to its male and female citizens.

summarizing statement

See Gathering Ideas and Information, page 15, and Organizing Your Writing, pages 18–21.

Writing to Persuade

Occasionally, people write to persuade others to think or feel the way they do about something. Persuasive writing may be in the form of an essay, a letter, a review, or a speech. The writer's opinion is usually but not always stated near the beginning. The opinion should be supported by evidence. Here are some things to think about as you write to persuade:

PREWRITING

Choosing a Topic

- **What issues do I feel strongly about?**

- **Is there a book I have read or a movie I have seen that I thought was especially good (or bad)?**

- **Do I know enough about this topic to persuade others to agree with my viewpoint?**

Gathering Information

- **What do I already know?**

- **Where can I find facts, reasons, and expert opinions to support my viewpoint?**

- **How does my audience feel about this topic?**

- **What forms of evidence will best appeal to my audience?**

DRAFTING

- What major points do I wish to make?

- In what order should I arrange my ideas?

RESPONDING AND REVISING

- Is my thesis statement—the statement of my main idea—strong and clear?

- Have I organized my ideas in an effective order?

- Have I included enough evidence to support my opinion?

- Have I cut irrelevant material?

PROOFREADING

- Did I divide my writing into paragraphs properly?

- Have I used correct punctuation and capitalization?

PUBLISHING

- Should I include any visuals?

- Should I make this a written or an oral presentation?

PERSUASIVE WRITING MODELS

Persuasive Essay, page 80

Persuasive Letter, page 81

Book Review, page 82

Movie Review, page 83

Speech with Visuals, pages 84–85

MODEL: PERSUASIVE ESSAY

*In a **persuasive essay**, the writer tries to convince an audience of his or her opinion on a particular topic. A good persuasive essay uses logic to support its argument.*

Soccer Is Here to Stay

thesis statement

It should be clear to everyone at Baker Middle School that we should add soccer to our list of intermural sports. Soccer is not just a passing fad. It is here to stay.

logical support
for opinion

At one time, soccer was unpopular in our country. Today, however, you can see it more and more often on television. It has always been popular in Europe, South America, and Asia. Many students at our school have cultural backgrounds from these parts of the world. Quite a few of them have expressed a desire to play soccer, but our school has no team for them to join.

Soccer is a game that involves fancy footwork, steady nerves, and stamina. It is fun to play and fun to watch. If we start a soccer team at Baker, nearly half the school will turn out to cheer the team on. Baker knows that soccer is here to stay.

See Adding Details and Examples, page 27.

*The purpose of a **persuasive letter** is to express an opinion and to convince someone else of the validity of your opinion. A persuasive letter can be to a person, a group, a business, or a publication. A letter to the editor of a local newspaper is a common example of persuasive writing.*

14 Clover Lane
Freeville, NY 13068
March 3, 199–

Editor
Freeville Express
386 Main Street
Freeville, NY 13068

Dear Editor:

thesis statement

    Your recent articles on the fires at Hayes Department Store and Memorial Hospital lead to one conclusion: Freeville needs its own volunteer fire department. The firefighters from Middletown and Upper Meadow deserve our praise and

supporting details

gratitude. However, our town is now large enough to bear the responsibility for its own safety. Furthermore, fire-fighting services could be delivered more efficiently if personnel and equipment did not have to travel the extra miles from these other towns. What can be more important than providing for the safety of our families?

Sincerely,

Howard Sutfin

Howard Sutfin

See Writing for Others, page 38.

MODEL: BOOK REVIEW

A **book review** gives an opinion about a book the writer has read. It supports that opinion with details from the book.

title
author

summary

opinion

Journey to the Center of the Earth by Jules Verne is the exciting story of three daring explorers. They travel to Iceland and enter an extinct volcano. Once inside, they travel down toward the center of the earth. Along the way, they find prehistoric plants and an underground ocean, complete with hideous monsters. They make wonderful discoveries, but will they ever be able to return home?

Although this book was published more than one hundred years ago, it is still thrilling. If you like science fiction, you will enjoy *Journey to the Center of the Earth*.

See Titles, page 176.

*A **movie review** expresses the writer's opinion about a movie and supports that opinion with details from the movie.*

title

opinion

reasons

I do not understand why so many people like the movie <u>Day of the Dinosaurs</u>. Although the special effects are amazing, I think it is too skimpy on plot, too different from the book, and much too violent.

There is very little plot at all. The movie is one big car chase, except that some of the "cars" are dinosaurs. The book is much better at telling you what is happening and why. The movie concentrates on being scary. I think younger kids might have nightmares if they were allowed to see it on video.

If you like suspense—and dinosaurs—my advice is to read the book. If you love special effects, rent the movie and fast-forward past the boring parts.

See Titles, page 176.

MODEL: SPEECH WITH VISUALS

In speech-making, practice makes perfect.

A **speech** is an oral presentation. When the purpose of a speech is to persuade, the speaker expresses a particular viewpoint and tries to convince his or her listeners to agree.

Follow these tips when you prepare a speech:

- **Use note cards or an outline as a guide. Do not simply read your speech aloud.**

- **When possible, use visuals such as charts, diagrams, photographs, or slides to help make your point and to capture your audience's attention.**

When you present your speech to an audience, remember these tips:

- **Speak clearly and loudly enough to be heard. Pace yourself so that you do not speak too quickly or too slowly.**

- **Look up from your notes frequently, and look at your audience. Your listeners need to feel that you are speaking directly to them.**

- **Introduce your visuals, and explain them clearly.**

- **Thank your audience, and ask for questions.**

The following items show how a speaker might use notes to present an oral report.

We desperately need four-way stop signs at the intersection of Oak and Elm streets. As you can see by the map,…

thesis statement

I. *Needed: four-way stop signs at Oak and Elm*
   A. Intersection is dangerous (show map)
   B. Children cross to and from Oak Park School
   C. Three accidents (show clippings)

reference to visuals

Four-way stop signs will save lives. We have them at Pine and Maple streets, and we have had no accidents there….

II. *Save lives*
   A. No accidents at Pine and Maple
   B. Slows traffic to safe speed

support for opinion

This investment is worth the money. One of these days, an accident victim will sue the town. The proposed signs will cost less than a lawsuit. Besides, we cannot put a price on the safety of children….

III. *Worth the money*
   A. Less than lawsuit
   B. Saving lives more important

See Adding Details and Examples, page 27.

PERSUASIVE/EXPOSITORY WRITING

Everyday Writing

Most people write at least a little every day. On the job, people write business letters and complete forms. At home, they take messages, send letters, and write in their journals. At school, they take notes and write summaries. Everyday writing can be very informal. Nevertheless, following certain steps in the writing process may help you organize and focus your writing.

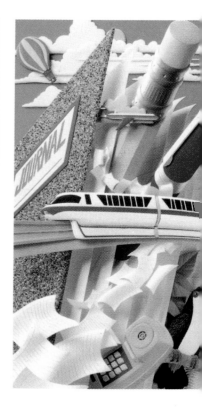

PREWRITING

Choosing a Topic

- **What is the main idea of this message, letter, or set of notes?**

- **Am I writing for myself or for others?**

Gathering Information

- **Should I freewrite to let my ideas flow?**

- **What information do I need before I begin to write?**

DRAFTING

- What is the most important point I wish to make?
- How should I organize my writing?

RESPONDING AND REVISING

- Have I said everything I meant to say?
- If I am writing for somebody else, will that person understand what I have written?

PROOFREADING

- Should I spell out any abbreviations?
- Have I used correct punctuation?

PUBLISHING

- Am I sharing my writing with someone or keeping it for myself?
- Should I make a neater copy of my writing?

EVERYDAY WRITING MODELS

Personal Journal, page 88

Dialogue Journal, page 89

Writer's Notebook, page 90

Messages, page 91

Friendly Letter, page 92

Business Letter, page 93

Forms, pages 94–95

Note Taking, page 96

Summary, page 97

MODEL: PERSONAL JOURNAL

A writer's **personal journal** is a place to record thoughts, dreams, ideas, responses to literature, or anything else that strikes a writer's fancy.

date of entry

informal language, including sentence fragments and abbreviations

January 8, 199-

A dreary, gray day. I woke up late—we're still on vacation! I thought about writing a letter to Angus, but instead I went up into the attic. Found my old copy of <u>The Phantom Tollbooth</u>. What a great book! I would like to write like Norton Juster.

Whoops! Here are my New Year's resolutions, a few days late:

1. Clean room more often.
2. Go to library weekly.
3. Be <u>a little</u> nicer to P., even if he is sometimes the world's worst brother.

See Writing for Yourself, page 38.

*A **dialogue journal** is a conversation in writing between a student and a teacher. Usually, the conversation is about something learned in class.*

March 11, 199-

Mrs. Zarkov,

When we talk about square roots, I get confused. I keep mixing up the square of a number with the square root of a number. Is there any good way to keep this straight? I would have done better on the homework if I hadn't been confused.

Kevin

speaking directly to teacher

Kevin,

I knew there was something wrong, and I'm glad you clued me in. Maybe if you remember that the root of a word is a small part of a word, you can recall that a square root is a small part, or a factor, of a number. A square is a product. Try it!

Mrs. Zarkov

responding directly to writing

See Writing to Learn, page 36.

MODEL: WRITER'S NOTEBOOK

In a **writer's notebook,** a writer keeps ideas for writing. These might include sketches and clippings, as well as lists, words, reflections, and reminders.

heading

lists

Ideas for Poems

the way leaves fall—spiraling, wafting, drifting, floating, sinking, whirling

—Look at Emily Dickinson's poems again.—

OR

comments

something about gardening
planting? turn over—sow—sprout
rhymes for plant: can't, chant, pant, rant
rhymes for garden: harden, yard in????
(not very good rhymes!)

See Writing for Yourself, page 38.

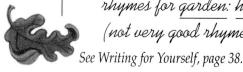

*Taking **phone messages** requires speed, accuracy, and thoroughness. A good message tells the receiver all he or she needs to know.*

date and time

receiver of message

name of caller

detailed message

signature

2:00 P.M. Friday

Dad—

Dr. Ng's office called to confirm your appointment on Tuesday afternoon at 4:00. Call 555-9090 if you can't go.

Greta

To *Ms. Landfear*

Date *1/15/9-*   Time *4:00*   A.M. / (P.M.)

WHILE YOU WERE OUT

M *r. Alvarez*

Of *Folker Books*

Phone *(212) 555-7800*

Telephoned	✓	Please call	
Called to see you		Will call again	
Returned your call		Urgent	

Message *He wants to order 4 more copies of The Little Mermaid.*

Jay

See Writing for Others, page 38.

MODEL: FRIENDLY LETTER

One of the most common forms of everyday writing is the **friendly letter.** A writer may send letters for any purpose: to entertain and express, to describe, to inform, or to persuade.

heading

> 2480 Kimbark Ave.
> Chicago, IL 60637
> June 4, 199—

greeting

Dear Augie,

body

It was great to see you at the team picnic. Everybody was glad you came. Since you moved away, we haven't kept in touch the way we should.

How are things going? Do you have a lot of new friends? I'm sure none of them can play first base as well as Mags or drop fly balls as often as Derek!

Please write back and tell me your plans for the summer. Maybe we can get together.

closing

Your friend,

signature

An-Li

See Writing for Others, page 38.

*A **business letter** is more formal than a friendly letter. It may be sent to inform, to persuade, or to request information.*

heading

40 Terrace Rd.
Fremont, CA 94539
May 28, 199–

inside address

Mr. Peter Decker
Decker Industries
717 Decker Court
Carmel, IN 46032

greeting

Dear Mr. Decker:

body

We are studying environmental issues at school, and I have learned that your company is on the cutting edge of recycling technology. Please send a catalog or a brochure about your recycled products to the address above. Thank you.

closing

Sincerely,

signature

Cal Ventura
Cal Ventura

return address

Cal Ventura
40 Terrace Rd.
Fremont, CA 94539

mailing address

Mr. Peter Decker
Decker Industries
717 Decker Court
Carmel, IN 46032

See Writing for Others, page 38.

M O D E L : F O R M S

Writers complete **forms** to join clubs and organizations, apply for jobs, order merchandise, return merchandise, and so on. Every form is different, so the only rules are these: Follow the directions, and write neatly!

neat handwriting

specific directions

DRYDEN PUBLIC LIBRARY
Application for Library Card

Name _____ *Valdez* _____ *Maria Elena* _____
              (last)   (first)
Address _____ *54 Yellow Barn Rd.* _____
              (Number and Street)
Dryden _____ *NY* _____ *13053* _____
(City)   (State)   (ZIP)
How long at this address? _*2 months*_

DO NOT WRITE BELOW THIS LINE
_____

_____ ID# _____ BY

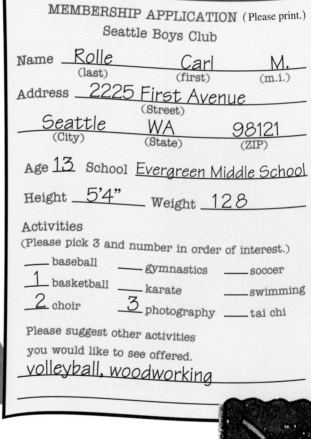

MEMBERSHIP APPLICATION (Please print.)
Seattle Boys Club

Name __Rolle__ __Carl__ __M.__
       (last)   (first)   (m.i.)

Address __2225 First Avenue__
             (Street)

__Seattle__ __WA__ __98121__
 (City)   (State)   (ZIP)

Age __13__ School __Evergreen Middle School__

Height __5'4"__ Weight __128__

Activities
(Please pick 3 and number in order of interest.)

___ baseball   ___ gymnastics   ___ soccer

__1__ basketball   ___ karate   ___ swimming

__2__ choir   __3__ photography   ___ tai chi

Please suggest other activities
you would like to see offered.
__volleyball, woodworking__

MODEL: NOTE TAKING

Note taking is paraphrasing or rewriting oral or written material in one's own words, usually in a shortened form. You can take notes to study for tests or to prepare oral or written presentations.

ORIGINAL MATERIAL

European explorers searched for a northwest passage through and around North America to reach the wealth of Asia. John Cabot believed he had found one when he landed at Newfoundland in 1497. Thirty years later, Giovanni da Verrazano searched the coastline from the Carolinas to Newfoundland. In the 1530s, Jacques Cartier found the St. Lawrence River and sailed up it in search of Asia. Henry Hudson did the same with the Hudson River in 1609.

Notes

paraphrased main ideas

Hunt for a northwest passage to Asia

1497: Cabot (Newfoundland)
1527: Verrazano (up East Coast)
1530s: Cartier (St. Lawrence)
1609: Hudson (Hudson River)

page references

source: America the Beautiful, pp. 130–131

WRITING TO LEARN

A **summary** is a condensed version of written material. It contains main ideas and facts rewritten in the summarizer's own words.

ORIGINAL MATERIAL

George Gershwin was born in Brooklyn, New York, in 1898 to Russian immigrant parents. He studied piano from the age of 14 and wrote his first hit song in 1919. He then proceeded to write hit after hit for Broadway musicals. However, he always loved classical music, which he wrote with a jazz flair. He wrote a string quartet called Lullaby in 1919 and the beautiful Rhapsody in Blue in 1924. Among his most famous classical works are the opera Porgy and Bess and the orchestral tone poem An American in Paris.

Summary

main idea

major points
paraphrased

George Gershwin was a composer of classical music as well as Broadway songs. He achieved early success writing for Broadway musicals and wrote the classical works Rhapsody in Blue, Porgy and Bess, and An American in Paris.

Writing for a Test

Writing for a test requires special skills. Usually the writer has no choice of topic; the topic is assigned. Often there is a time limit during which all stages of the writing process must be carried out. Keeping in mind any such restrictions, you should build in the time to plan and revise your writing. Thinking about these questions may help:

PREWRITING

Choosing a Topic

- **What questions must I answer?**

- **Am I being asked to compare, give an opinion, explain, analyze, or describe?**

- **What kind of writing will fulfill this assignment?**

Gathering Information

- **Am I allowed to refer to my textbook?**

- **Can I make a rough outline to help organize my thoughts?**

DRAFTING

- What will I use as my topic sentence?

- How much time do I have to finish the draft? How many minutes should I allot to each question or essay?

RESPONDING AND REVISING

- Have I answered the question completely?

- Are there any additional facts I should include?

PROOFREADING

- Have I spelled every word correctly?

- Are my sentences grammatically correct?

PUBLISHING

- Do I have time to rewrite this neatly?

TEST WRITING MODELS

Essay Questions, page 100

Writing to Prompts, pages 101–102

MODEL: ESSAY QUESTIONS

Many tests include **essay questions**. *The test taker must divide the given time into time to plan, time to draft, and time to revise each answer.*

think/plan—5 min.
write—12 min.
check—3 min.

freewrite facts and ideas

organize by numbering facts in logical order

develop main idea for topic

write

2. Question (20 minutes): How did Native Americans adapt to their environment? Give two examples.

Inuit—igloos, travel for food   2
Iroquois—homes of wood and bark,
hunted game   1
topic sentence: Native Americans had to adapt their housing and eating habits to their environment.

2.   Native Americans had to adapt their housing and eating habits to their environment. The Iroquois lived in the Eastern forests, where trees and game animals were plentiful. They built houses called longhouses out of wood and bark. An example of adaptation to extreme conditions is the Inuit way of life. In the Arctic, many Inuit built igloos for winter homes. They, too, traveled in search of food.

See Understanding Task, Audience, and Purpose (TAP), page 14.

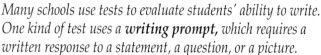

Many schools use tests to evaluate students' ability to write. One kind of test uses a **writing prompt**, which requires a written response to a statement, a question, or a picture. Careful reading of the prompt will help determine the writing form, the audience (if given), and the purpose for writing (to inform, to persuade, to entertain, to describe). Often students are supplied with enough paper to plan and write the response.

prompt

Some people say exercise not only keeps you fit but also can give you more energy and better concentration. Do you agree or disagree? Write an essay for your classmates in which you state your opinion and support it with at least one example.

Does exercise keep me fit, boost my energy, and help me concentrate? Yes. Example of this: my swimming

organizing notes

Reasons why (or how?) it helps:
1. the exercise gives me energy
2. easier to concentrate when
*   I've exercised*

thesis statement

Frequent exercise can help improve your energy level and concentration.

(continued on page 102)

Writing for a Test

title	*Exercise: What They Say Is True*
thesis statement	Can exercise not only keep you fit but improve your concentration and increase your energy? From my experience with swimming, I certainly think so.
example	Sometimes I feel too tired to go to swim team practice after school, but I go anyway because it's more than just physical activity. After practice, I am
support for opinion	ready to go home, eat, study, play with my little brother, and climb Mount Everest! I feel very energetic after a good workout.
	Immediately after practice, I am usually tired. As soon as I eat a snack, however, I am ready for the second half of my day! It seems so much easier to study, because my mind can focus on what I'm doing.
call to action	When you hear people say they feel better when they exercise, it's probably true. Try it yourself for a while, and see how much better you feel about school and yourself.

Grammar, Usage, and Mechanics

Grammar

Sentences 104
Nouns 123
Pronouns 130
Adjectives 138
Verbs 146
Adverbs 160
Prepositions 164

Usage 168

Mechanics

Punctuation 172
Titles 176
Abbreviations 177

SENTENCES

SENTENCE·

A *sentence* is a group of words that expresses a complete thought. A sentence names someone or something and tells what that person or thing is or does. Every sentence begins with a capital letter and ends with an end mark.

My father travels around the country.

Has the airplane landed?

What amazing places your mind can take you!

The following word groups are not sentences because they do not express complete thoughts.

the strangeness of the earth's oceans

could even travel back in time or visit other planets

with or without a ticket or passport

GRAMMAR

Exercise 1

Tell whether each group of words is a *sentence* or *not a sentence.*

1. Maria has been telling Hakim an amazing story.
2. It is *Fantastic Voyage,* a movie.
3. To save a dying man.
4. Scientists are shrunk to microscopic size.
5. A tiny submarine.
6. Into a world of unimagined complexity and beauty.
7. Dangers await these brave voyagers.
8. Through the valves of a beating heart.
9. Fortunately, the operation was a complete success.
10. At the last minute, through the patient's tear duct.
11. A remarkable story indeed.
12. Time travel sounds more interesting to me.
13. My imagination shows me the signing of the Declaration of Independence.
14. All the way back to the times of the dinosaurs.
15. Together, we might find many new friends in those long-ago times and places.

For additional practice, turn to page 180.

Writing Application

Brainstorm ideas for sentences about an unusual place or time to visit. Then write ten sentences about your imaginary travels. Share your sentences.

SENTENCES

DECLARATIVE SENTENCE

A *declarative sentence* makes a statement. Use a period (.) at the end of a declarative sentence.

Janelle is painting a picture of an imaginary place.

She has placed three moons in the evening sky.

INTERROGATIVE SENTENCE

An *interrogative sentence* asks a question. Use a question mark (?) at the end of an interrogative sentence.

Who could ever create a more imaginative scene?

Did she dream it up by herself?

Exercise 2

Tell whether each sentence is *declarative* or *interrogative*. Then name the mark of punctuation that should end the sentence.

1. Abiko has challenged me to a contest
2. Which one of us can create the most imaginative painting
3. Now, where did I put my watercolor paints
4. Abiko has started painting with enthusiasm
5. Before long, his canvas is filled with color
6. Should I paint more quickly

EXCLAMATORY SENTENCE

An *exclamatory sentence* expresses strong feeling. Use an exclamation point (!) at the end of an exclamatory sentence.

What fantastic places those are!

How I want to visit all of them!

INTERJECTION

An *interjection* is a word or a group of words that expresses strong feeling.

Aha! Hooray! Of course! Oh, no! Yikes!

You can separate an interjection from the rest of a sentence with either an exclamation point or a comma, depending on the strength of the feeling.

***Hey,* is that your painting?**

***Wow!* That's really amazing!**

Writing Application

Write an ad for a travel service called Imaginative Journeys, Inc. Use declarative and interrogative sentences in your ad. Share your ad, and see who asks for tickets!

SENTENCES

IMPERATIVE SENTENCE

An *imperative sentence* gives a command or makes a request. Use a period (.) at the end of an imperative sentence.

Think about all the uses for artwork.

Please show my uncle your painting.

The subject of an imperative sentence is *you* (understood).

(you) Talk to Uncle Ray.

(you) Let him put your painting on a greeting card.

Exercise 3

Tell whether each sentence is *exclamatory* or *imperative.* Then name the mark of punctuation that should end the sentence.

1. Please come into this bookstore with me

2. What a variety of books is here

3. How much money I could spend on them

4. Now, take a look at the covers of these science fiction novels

5. Wow, Abiko, those two covers look like some of my paintings

For additional practice, turn to pages 180–181.

COMPLETE SUBJECT AND COMPLETE PREDICATE

Every sentence is made up of two parts, a subject and a predicate.

The *complete subject* includes all the words that tell whom or what the sentence is about.

The *complete predicate* includes all the words that tell what the subject of the sentence is or does.

Complete Subject	Complete Predicate
My two older brothers	stared at me silently.
I	blinked.

Exercise 4

Identify the complete subject and the complete predicate of each sentence.

1. My brothers are acting suspiciously.
2. Jaime took a letter out of the mailbox yesterday.
3. The contents of that letter mystify me.
4. Two classmates of mine whispered behind my back.
5. This secret is fun for everyone except me.

Writing Application

Brainstorm ideas for a fantastic birthday party. Write several sentences about the party. Underline the complete subject and the complete predicate of each sentence.

SENTENCES

SIMPLE SUBJECT AND SIMPLE PREDICATE

The *simple subject* is the main word or words in the complete subject. Sometimes the complete subject and the simple subject are the same.

The *simple predicate* is the main word or words in the complete predicate. Sometimes the complete predicate and the simple predicate are the same.

In the following sentences, the simple subjects and the simple predicates are underlined.

Complete Subject	Complete Predicate
<u>Everyone</u> in my house	<u>is keeping</u> a secret.
<u>Grandma Lopez</u>	<u>says</u> nothing to me.
(<u>you</u>)	<u>Ask</u> her about it.

Exercise 5

Identify the *simple subject* and the *simple predicate* of each sentence.

1. The secret was revealed on Saturday afternoon.
2. My relatives from near and far arrived on my birthday.
3. Even Aunt Maria came.
4. I had a wonderful, fantastic party.

For additional practice, turn to pages 182–185.

LOOKING AT LANGUAGE

I am from Moscow, the capital city of Russia. I came to the United States so I could learn English. I hope I can use both English and Russian when I am older.

In Russian, we use an alphabet that is very different from the English alphabet. It has 33 letters and looks like this:

АБВГДЕЁЖЗИЙКЛМНОП
РСТУФХЦЧШЩЪЫЬЭЮЯ

Many things are different for me here in the United States, including my name! In Russian, my name looks like

Ксениа

and sounds like [kəs•yen´ē´ə]. But here, I have chosen to be called *Roxanne*. It is a more American name, and people will be able to say it more easily.

111

GRAMMAR

SENTENCES

COMPOUND SUBJECT

A *compound subject* consists of two or more subjects that have the same predicate. The simple subjects in a compound subject are usually joined by *and* or *or*.

The craters and plains of the moon have had no human visitors for some time.

If there are three or more simple subjects in a compound subject, use commas to separate them.

Darryl Harris, Setsu Wanatabe, and I will present a report about that mission.

COMPOUND PREDICATE

A *compound predicate* consists of two or more predicates that have the same subject. The simple predicates in a compound predicate are usually joined by *and* or *or*.

We will find the card catalog or will ask the librarian for help.

If there are three or more simple predicates in a compound predicate, use commas to separate them.

The three of us whispered, pointed, and made notes.

Exercise 6

Tell whether each sentence has a *compound subject* or a *compound predicate*. Then identify the simple subjects in each compound subject and the simple predicates in each compound predicate.

1. In 1969, *Apollo 11* and *Apollo 12* placed the first humans on the moon's surface.

2. Twelve astronauts walked or drove across the dusty moonscape during the three and a half years of moon landings.

3. They took soil samples, measured temperatures, and tested the lunar gravity.

4. Setsu, Darryl, or I will find a photograph of an "earthrise."

5. Eugene A. Cernan and Harrison H. Schmitt rode in the last Apollo lunar module.

6. Back in orbit, they released the lunar module and measured the vibrations from its impact.

7. *Apollo 17*'s return to earth brought the mission to a close and marked the end of manned moon landings.

For additional practice, turn to pages 186–187.

Writing Application

Imagine visiting the moon. Write and share a paragraph about what you and other visitors could do there. Use at least one compound subject and one compound predicate.

SENTENCES

SIMPLE SENTENCE

A *simple sentence* expresses only one complete thought.

Objects from space fall into the atmosphere.

The subject or the predicate of a simple sentence may be simple or compound.

Subject	Predicate
Some <u>meteors</u>	<u>grow</u> hot and <u>burn</u> up.
<u>Metal</u> or <u>stone</u>	sometimes <u>reaches</u> the ground.

COMPOUND SENTENCE

A *compound sentence* is made up of two or more simple sentences. The simple sentences usually are joined by a comma (,) and a *coordinating conjunction*—which is a connecting word such as *and, or,* or *but*—or by a semicolon (;).

Friction makes meteors incredibly hot<u>, and</u> they burn up miles above the earth's surface.

Some large meteors do not burn up completely<u>;</u> they are called meteorites.

A simple sentence within a compound sentence may have a compound subject or a compound predicate or both.

Meteors and meteorites fall<u>, and</u> they sparkle and glow.

GRAMMAR

Two common errors in sentence writing are the *run-on sentence* and the *comma splice*. **Run-on sentence** describes two simple sentences that are joined without punctuation. **Comma splice** describes two simple sentences that are joined with only a comma.

RUN-ON SENTENCE: A crater can be formed by a bomb it can be formed by a meteorite.

COMMA SPLICE: A crater can be formed by a bomb, it can be formed by a meteorite.

CORRECT: A crater can be formed by a bomb, or it can be formed by a meteorite.

Exercise 7

Identify each sentence as a *simple sentence* or a *compound sentence*.

1. Have you seen the Meteor Crater in Arizona?

2. This huge hole measures about 4,150 feet across and about 570 feet deep.

3. A meteorite crashed there perhaps 50,000 years ago, or it may have fallen even earlier.

4. In 1908, a meteorite streaked across the Siberian sky; people could see it for hundreds of miles.

5. Did it really weigh hundreds of tons?

6. In 1947, another meteorite exploded over Siberia; it created more than 200 craters.

For additional practice, turn to pages 188–189.

Writing Application

Could a meteorite fall into your schoolyard? Write several simple and compound sentences about the event. See who comes up with the wildest story!

SENTENCES

CLAUSE

A *clause* is a group of words that has a subject and a predicate. Some clauses can stand alone as sentences; others cannot. In these sentences, look for the subject and the predicate in each underlined clause.

Everyone should know about medical emergencies.

You can read first-aid manuals, or you can take special classes.

Although my aunt doesn't have a medical degree, she saved someone's life.

PHRASE

A *phrase* is a group of words that work together. A phrase does not have both a subject and a predicate.

Amy watched Eric from the kitchen window.

Eric was playing in the yard.

Exercise 8

Identify each underlined group of words as a *phrase* or a *clause*.

1. An hour or so passed <u>while Eric played outside.</u>

2. He worked <u>in his construction site</u>; then he climbed <u>on the woodpile.</u>

3. Suddenly Aunt Amy heard a cry and the sound <u>of Eric's footsteps.</u>

4. With one look <u>at his tear-streaked face</u>, <u>she ran to</u> the medicine cabinet.

5. <u>When she examined the wound</u>, Aunt Amy immediately bundled Eric <u>into the car</u> and rushed him <u>to the emergency room.</u>

6. <u>After he examined Eric</u>, the doctor said, "You have been bitten <u>by an insect.</u>"

For additional practice, turn to pages 190–191.

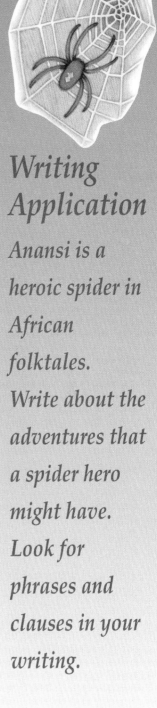

Writing Application

Anansi is a heroic spider in African folktales. Write about the adventures that a spider hero might have. Look for phrases and clauses in your writing.

SENTENCES

INDEPENDENT CLAUSE

An *independent clause* expresses a complete thought and can stand alone as a simple sentence.

Some pollution affects our homes and schools.

If their neighbors cooperate, <u>young people and adults can clean up their neighborhoods.</u>

Another way to think of a compound sentence is to look at it as two or more independent clauses.

<u>Toxic waste is hard to clean up</u>, and <u>it can be a deadly form of pollution.</u>

DEPENDENT CLAUSE

A *dependent clause* (also called a *subordinate clause*) contains a subject and a predicate, but it does not express a complete thought and it cannot stand alone.

A dependent clause often begins with a *subordinating conjunction*, which is a connecting word, such as *after, although, because, before, if, since, when,* or *while*—or with the pronoun *that* or *which.*

In these sentences, the dependent clause is underlined.

People became more sensitive to pollution problems <u>after they learned about toxic waste.</u>

<u>If we want pollution-free neighborhoods</u>, shouldn't we work together?

Notice that the part that is <u>not</u> underlined can stand alone.

Exercise 9

Tell whether the underlined group of words in each sentence is an *independent clause* or a *dependent clause*. If it is a dependent clause, write the subordinating conjunction that connects it with the rest of the sentence.

1. If you go to New York City, consider a visit to Brooklyn.

2. Fifteen teenagers there gained some fame because they were pollution fighters.

3. They called themselves the Toxic Avengers, a name borrowed from a pollution-fighting superhero.

4. Although it was located next to a school, the Radiac Research Corporation was storing large amounts of medical waste.

5. The Toxic Avengers heard about this and planned a response.

6. When a crowd gathered for a public rally, the teens told the people about Radiac.

7. Public awareness grew after the rally was held.

For additional practice, turn to page 190.

Writing Application

Write and share a brief news article about a real or an imaginary neighborhood hero. Use independent clauses and dependent clauses in your article.

SENTENCES

COMPLEX SENTENCE

A *complex sentence* consists of an independent clause and at least one dependent clause. Dependent clauses often tell *why, when, where, what,* or *which one.*

> *A dependent clause that begins a sentence is usually followed by a comma.*

<u>Because someone had been careless with matches</u>, a fire started at the Johnsons' home last week.
>   (tells why)

> *A dependent clause that comes at the end of the sentence is usually not preceded by a comma.*

Smoke filled the house <u>as firefighters arrived.</u>
>   (tells when)

Volunteers soon set up a command post <u>where we were standing.</u>
>   (tells where)

The chief said <u>that we all should step back.</u>
>   (tells what)

> *When a dependent clause comes in the middle of a sentence, it is usually set off by commas.*

The fire, <u>which we saw spreading rapidly,</u> shot sparks into the sky.
>   (tells which one)

GRAMMAR

Exercise 10

Tell whether each sentence is a *compound sentence* or a *complex sentence.*

1. As she watched the fire, the chief directed the firefighters.
2. Outside, the atmosphere was tense; all of us worried about the firefighters' safety and the Johnsons' rescue.
3. When they all walked out, most of us cheered and waved.
4. The fire looked bad to me, but the house was repaired fairly quickly.

Exercise 11

Add a dependent clause to each independent clause to make a complex sentence. The dependent clause that you create should begin with the subordinating conjunction in parentheses ( ).

1. volunteer firefighters respond *(when)*
2. they need special training *(since)*
3. they often must work *(where)*
4. volunteer firefighters get my vote of thanks *(because)*

For additional practice, turn to pages 192–193.

For additional practice, turn to pages 192–193.

Writing Application

Brainstorm ideas about ways in which volunteers help others. Write a poem or song about one of your ideas. Use at least two complex sentences.

Looking at Language

ATTILA ELTETO ON HUNGARIAN

I am from Budapest, the capital of Hungary. Hungary is a country in eastern Europe, between Austria and Romania.

There are many differences between Hungarian and English. Some differences make learning English easier, and some make learning it harder. One thing that I miss in Hungarian is the word *tessék* [tesh´āk]. In Hungary, *tessék* is used to mean many different things. For example:

Phrase	When Used
Come in!	when answering the door
Hello!	when answering the phone
Here you are.	when giving something to someone else
Can I help you?	when greeting a customer
Sit here.	when indicating a seat
Excuse me?	when asking someone to repeat something

I will have to learn many English phrases just to cover this one Hungarian word!

NOUNS

NOUN

A *noun* is a word that names a person, a place, a thing, or an idea. In these examples, notice that some nouns start with a capital letter and that some nouns are made up of more than one word.

Person		Place	
Grandma	friend	forest	Mt. Hood
brother	lifeguard	seashore	Sahara Desert
Sam Rios	Dr. Evans	kitchen	field

Thing		Idea	
computer	kitten	joy	Federalism
elephant	lightning	courage	memory
half dollar	elbow	love	anger

Exercise 12

Identify the nouns in these sentences. Tell whether each noun names a *person*, a *place*, a *thing*, or an *idea*.

1. Kim is reading a book about a detective.
2. The hero, Marla Franklin, loves mystery and adventure.
3. Marla and her family are on vacation at Lake Tahoe.

For additional practice, turn to pages 194–195.

For additional practice, turn to pages 194–195.

Writing Application

Choose any noun from Exercise 12. Use it to begin a word web. Add to the web ideas of your own. How many nouns are in your finished word web?

NOUNS

COMMON NOUN

A *common noun* names any person, place, thing, or idea. It begins with a lowercase letter.

school	octopus	scientist	anger
pizza	document	country	politician
diamond	opinion	organization	street
movie	month	broccoli	poem
writer	park	religion	villain

PROPER NOUN

A *proper noun* names a particular person, place, thing, or idea. Begin each important word in a proper noun with a capital letter.

November	Amelia Earhart Boulevard
Adams Middle School	Declaration of Independence
Walter de la Mare	"Paul Revere's Ride"
Beauty and the Beast	Christianity
Chicago	Katmai National Park
Sierra Club	Sojourner Truth

Exercise 13

Identify the *common nouns* and the *proper nouns* in each sentence.

1. Rani said, "The bravest people in the world are doctors."
2. "My stepbrother has been working in India since March."
3. Ben asked, "Does Tom work at a hospital?"
4. "No," Rani replied. "Tom is the doctor at a clinic in Agra."

Exercise 14

Proper nouns give more precise information than common nouns do. Rewrite these sentences. Replace each underlined noun phrase with a proper noun.

5. My friend shows courage everywhere she goes.
6. When the organization went to a state last spring, my friend saved the life of a drowning swimmer at a lake.
7. In a month, she found my dog when he was lost.
8. Maybe someday she'll star in an adventure film like a movie.

For additional practice, turn to page 194.

For additional practice, turn to page 194.

Writing Application

Brainstorm ideas for a character sketch about someone you consider brave. Use at least four common nouns and four proper nouns in your character sketch.

125

GRAMMAR

NOUNS

SINGULAR NOUN

A *singular noun* names one person, place, or thing.

building	bus	dish	decoy
potato	story	chief	waltz
stereo	switch	box	community

PLURAL NOUN

A *plural noun* names more than one person, place, or thing. Make most nouns plural by adding -*s* or -*es*. The *y* at the end of some words changes to *i* first.

buildings	buses	dishes	decoys
potatoes	stories	chiefs	waltzes
stereos	switches	boxes	communities

Some nouns change their spelling in the plural form.

calf, calves   tooth, teeth   child, children

Exercise 15

Give the plural form for each singular noun and the singular form for each plural noun.

1. bush	4. woman	7. watches	10. gases
2. lice	5. suitcase	8. melody	11. cranberry
3. butterflies	6. turkey	9. cheeses	12. scarf

For additional practice, turn to page 195.

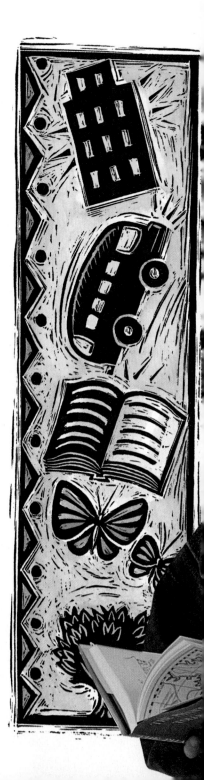

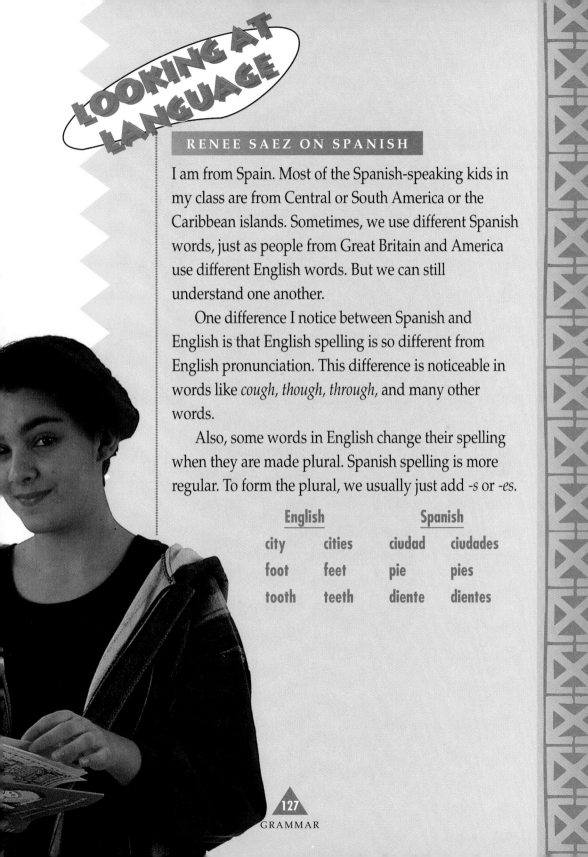

LOOKING AT LANGUAGE

RENEE SAEZ ON SPANISH

I am from Spain. Most of the Spanish-speaking kids in my class are from Central or South America or the Caribbean islands. Sometimes, we use different Spanish words, just as people from Great Britain and America use different English words. But we can still understand one another.

One difference I notice between Spanish and English is that English spelling is so different from English pronunciation. This difference is noticeable in words like *cough*, *though*, *through*, and many other words.

Also, some words in English change their spelling when they are made plural. Spanish spelling is more regular. To form the plural, we usually just add *-s* or *-es*.

English		Spanish	
city	cities	ciudad	ciudades
foot	feet	pie	pies
tooth	teeth	diente	dientes

NOUNS

POSSESSIVE NOUN

A *possessive noun* shows ownership or possession. An apostrophe (') is used to form a possessive noun.

How many of you have heard of the acting career of Robert Coates?

How many of you have heard of Robert Coates's acting career?

Coates may have been the worst actor in America.

Coates may have been America's worst actor.

Exercise 16

Replace the underlined groups of words in these sentences with possessive nouns.

1. Charles Green was <u>the worst balloonist in Britain</u>.

2. With <u>the help of a colleague</u>, he prepared for flight.

3. Suddenly, <u>the ropes of the balloon</u> slipped off.

4. How surprised <u>the citizens of Cheltingham</u> must have been to hear <u>the calls for help from the flyers</u>!

SINGULAR POSSESSIVE NOUN

A *singular possessive noun* shows ownership by one person or thing. To form the possessive of most singular nouns, add an apostrophe (') and *-s*.

person   **a person's adventures**

PLURAL POSSESSIVE NOUN

A *plural possessive noun* shows ownership by more than one person or thing. To form the possessive of a plural noun that ends in *-s*, add an apostrophe (').

campers   **the campers' story**

To form the possessive of a plural noun that does not end in *-s*, add an apostrophe (') and *-s*.

mice   **the mice's escape route**

Exercise 17
Tell the *singular possessive* form of each noun.

1. artist   **2.** hour

Exercise 18
Tell the *plural possessive* form of each noun.

1. hostesses   **2.** teachers

For additional practice, turn to pages 196–197.

129

GRAMMAR

PRONOUNS

PRONOUN

A *pronoun* is a word that takes the place of one or more than one noun. Pronouns show number and gender. **Number** tells whether a pronoun is singular or plural. **Gender** tells whether a pronoun is masculine, feminine, or neuter. In this example, *He* is singular and masculine; *her* is singular and feminine; and *them* is plural and neuter.

Bill McCoy heard	**He** heard
a librarian tell	**her** tell
stories.	**them.**

A singular pronoun replaces a singular noun. A plural pronoun replaces a plural noun or two or more nouns that work together. The most common pronouns are the *personal pronouns.*

Singular	Plural
I, me, my, mine	we, us, our, ours
you, your, yours	you, your, yours
he, him, his,	they, them, their, theirs
she, her, hers,	
it, its	

Exercise 19

Identify the *personal pronouns* in these sentences.
Tell the number and gender of each one.

1. Leon asked Anne to tell him about some of her favorite books.

2. "OK," Anne told him. She chose some books and opened them.

3. "Here are biographies of women pioneers. I could talk about one of them."

4. Leon told her to pick one.

5. He enjoyed it.

For additional practice, turn to pages 198–199.

For additional practice, turn to pages 198–199.

Writing Application

Write a paragraph about a book you like. Use at least four personal pronouns in your paragraph. Then share your paragraph.

PRONOUNS

SUBJECT PRONOUN

A *subject pronoun* takes the place of the subject of a sentence.

I, you, he, she, it, we, and *they* are subject pronouns. Always capitalize the pronoun *I.*

I have been reading about Marie Dorion.

Subject pronouns often are combined with some verbs to form *contractions.*

In a pronoun-verb contraction, some of the letters in the verb are replaced with an apostrophe ('). These are some common pronoun-verb contractions.

I'm (I am)	**it's (it is)**
I'll (I will)	**we're (we are)**
you're (you are)	**they're (they are)**
you'll (you will)	**they'll (they will)**

OBJECT PRONOUN

An *object pronoun* takes the place of a noun that follows an action verb, such as *see* or *tell.*

Me, you, him, her, it, us, and *them* are object pronouns.

When Marie accompanied the trappers to Oregon, they showed her great respect.

Object pronouns are also used after prepositions, such as *about, at, by, for, from, to,* and *with.*

Marie loved Pierre Dorion and traveled with him.

REFLEXIVE PRONOUN

A *reflexive pronoun* refers to the subject of a sentence. *Myself, yourself, himself, herself, itself, ourselves, yourselves,* and *themselves* are reflexive pronouns.

One day, Marie found <u>herself</u> alone in the quiet forest.

Exercise 20

Replace the words in parentheses ( ) with pronouns. Tell whether each pronoun is a *subject,* an *object,* or a *reflexive* pronoun.

1. Marie Dorion untied the horse and loaded (the horse) with supplies.

2. As the three of (the survivors) left, Marie Dorion made (Marie Dorion) a promise—that (Marie Dorion and the children) would survive.

3. Nine days later, a snowstorm trapped (Marie Dorion) and the boys.

4. The Dorions kept (the Dorions) alive for fifty-three days.

5. Some Wallawalla Indians found Marie Dorion; (the Wallawallas) rescued (Marie Dorion) and the boys.

For additional practice, turn to pages 198–199.

For additional practice, turn to pages 198–199.

Writing Application

Write a paragraph about someone on an extraordinary journey. Use at least two subject pronouns, two object pronouns, and two reflexive pronouns. Share your paragraph.

PRONOUNS

PRONOUN– ANTECEDENT AGREEMENT

An *antecedent* is the noun or nouns to which a pronoun refers.

In 1847, Homan Walsh offered his help to some railway engineers.

The engineers were building a suspension bridge at Niagara Falls, and they were having trouble.

The antecedent is often in the same sentence as the pronoun. Sometimes, however, it is in another sentence.

Heavy cables had to cross a steep gorge. How to get them across was the problem.

A pronoun should agree with its antecedent in number and gender. More than one pronoun-antecedent combination can appear in a sentence.

Homan took a kite, and he attached a light rope to it.

A pronoun with more than one antecedent is plural, even if the antecedents differ in number or gender.

The chief engineer and his team looked on, and they were amazed.

Exercise 21

Tell the *antecedent* of each underlined pronoun.

1. Anna Taylor went to Niagara Falls, but she crossed it differently.
2. Witnesses watched with their mouths open.
3. Taylor squeezed herself into a barrel.
4. Was Taylor the first person to survive a trip over Niagara Falls? Of course she was!

Exercise 22

Tell the pronoun that is needed to complete each sentence. Also name the antecedent for each pronoun.

5. As president of the Senate in the 1830s, Martin Van Buren kept a gun near _____ to maintain order.
6. During the Civil War, Emma Edmonds spied for the Union after disguising _____ as a male slave.
7. Dr. Mary Walker, a surgeon, tended Union soldiers and spent time with some of _____ in a Confederate prison.

For additional practice, turn to pages 198–199.

For additional practice, turn to pages 198–199.

Writing Application

In what ways are you extraordinary? Write several sentences answering that question. Make sure that the pronouns you use agree with their antecedents.

PRONOUNS

A **possessive pronoun** shows ownership or possession. It takes the place of a possessive noun. *My, your, his, her, its, our,* and *their* are used before nouns.

Jerome and I are learning about our ancestors.

Mine, yours, his, hers, ours, and *theirs* stand alone.

This picture is his.

Be careful not to confuse a possessive pronoun with a contraction.

The picture shows Ashanti weavers at their looms; they're making beautiful *kente* cloth.

Exercise 23

Give the *possessive pronoun* that is needed to complete each sentence.

1. The Kung people use eggshells to store _____ water supply.

2. A Ndaka bride is carried to _____ wedding on a shaded platform; indeed, the day is almost entirely _____.

3. Jerome and I wonder whether _____ ancestors and _____ might have known each other.

For additional practice, turn to pages 200–201.

LOOKING AT LANGUAGE

QUYEN TU ON VIETNAMESE

I am from Vietnam, a country in Asia along the South China Sea. Many of the Vietnamese people who now live in America learned to speak both Vietnamese and French.

The Vietnamese language uses a different alphabet, with letters that look almost like English letters, except for the accent marks over them. These accent marks tell you the *tone* to use for the letters, which means the way to say the letters.

One hard thing to learn about English is that pronouns change form depending on how they are used. They can be used as subjects or as objects. In Vietnamese, we have only one form for each pronoun. It's like this:

English pronouns		Vietnamese pronouns
subject:	object:	subject or object:
I	me	toi
he	him	no
she	her	no

ADJECTIVES

An **adjective** is a word that modifies, or describes, a noun or a pronoun. Adjectives tell *what kind, how many,* or *which one.*

We saw a pride of <u>lazy</u> lions beneath a <u>shady</u> tree.
    what kind

<u>Three</u> adults and <u>four</u> cubs rested there.
    how many

The <u>smallest</u> cub was stalking an <u>older</u> brother.
    which one

Adjectives may come before or after the words they describe.

Most of the <u>powerful</u> <u>meat-eating</u> beasts ignored us.

A lioness, <u>calm</u> but <u>alert</u>, watched us pass by.

An adjective may also follow a linking verb, such as *is, seems,* or *appears.*

She seemed <u>harmless</u>; still, we were <u>careful</u>.

ARTICLE

The adjectives *a, an,* and *the* are called **articles.** The article *the* refers to a particular person, place, thing, or idea. The article *a* or *an* refers to any person, place, thing, or idea.

<u>The</u> leader gave <u>a</u> yawn.

138

GRAMMAR

Use *a* before a word that begins with a consonant sound.
Use *an* before a word that begins with a vowel sound.

a cub   a beautiful animal

an adventure   an energetic hunter

Exercise 24

Identify the *adjectives* and *articles* in the sentences. Tell the word that each adjective or article describes.

1. The lion is a sociable creature.
2. Cubs learn important skills at an early age.
3. Nightly hunts may provide rich feasts.
4. The yellow-brown coat of a lion is an effective camouflage.

Exercise 25

Use *adjectives* and *articles* to complete these sentences. Write the new sentences.

5. When _____ lion is _____, other animals must be _____.
6. _____ wildebeest or _____ antelope could become a _____ lion's dinner.
7. Then the pride, _____ and _____, might settle in for _____ nap.

For additional practice, turn to page 202.

For additional practice, turn to page 202.

Writing Application

Choose any animal from Exercise 25. Write and share a paragraph or poem about it. Use articles and interesting adjectives to describe the animal.

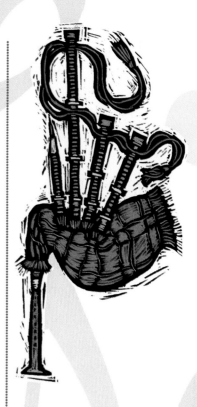

ADJECTIVES

PROPER ADJECTIVE

A *proper adjective* is formed from a proper noun. A proper adjective begins with a capital letter. Many proper adjectives describe nationality or location; some give other information.

African history   Scottish bagpipes

Republican candidate   Sioux traditions

Islamic law   Thai cuisine

Some proper adjectives are formed from people's names.

a Hemingway novel   the Lincoln years

Proper adjectives are formed in a variety of ways. If you are not sure how to form a particular proper adjective, look in a dictionary.

Exercise 26

Identify the *proper adjectives* in these sentences.

1. Albert Schweitzer was a European doctor and musician.

2. As a child, he attended German and French schools.

3. Schweitzer played organ concerts to fund an African hospital.

DEMONSTRATIVE ADJECTIVE

A *demonstrative adjective* points out a noun. It is more precise than an article, because it tells *which one*. The words *this, that, these,* and *those* are demonstrative adjectives.

This and *these* often refer to something nearby; *that* and *those* often refer to something farther away.

This book has more illustrations than that magazine.

Are those maps clear, or shall I look in these atlases?

Exercise 27

Identify the error or errors in each sentence.

1. Who collected all this African instruments?

2. That Kenyan drum is different from these Nigerian drum.

3. Can you play a melody on those one-stringed Ethiopian fiddle?

4. This kinds of instruments are called *kalimbas,* or "thumb pianos."

For additional practice, turn to page 202.

Writing Application

Brainstorm ideas for a trip around the world. Use proper adjectives to describe some of the sights and activities of your trip. Share your description.

ADJECTIVES

Adjectives can be used to compare nouns.

The *positive form* of an adjective is used when no comparison is being made.

old   wonderful   imaginative

How <u>old</u> the Inca empire seems to us today!

The *comparative form* of an adjective is used to compare two items. Form the comparative of most one-syllable adjectives by adding *-er.* For most adjectives with two or more syllables, add the word *more* before the adjective.

older   more wonderful   more imaginative

The Aztec empire is <u>older</u> than the Inca empire.

The *superlative form* of an adjective is used to compare three or more items. Form the superlative of most one-syllable adjectives by adding *-est.* For most adjectives with two or more syllables, add the word *most* before the adjective.

oldest   most wonderful   most imaginative

The Mayan empire is the <u>oldest</u> one in the Americas.

Exercise 28

Give the *comparative* and *superlative* forms of these adjectives.

1. sweet
2. rare
3. peaceful
4. dangerous
5. proud
6. reliable
7. hot
8. shiny

Exercise 29

Give the form of the *adjective* in parentheses ( ) that correctly completes each sentence.

9. The stone houses of wealthy Mayas looked (strong) and (impressive) than those of their poorer neighbors.
10. The clothing of Mayan priests was the (elaborate) of all.
11. The (beautiful) floating city of Tenochtitlán may have been the Aztecs' (great) achievement.
12. The Incas, who seem to have been (aggressive) than the Aztecs or Mayas, ruled the (large) empire in the hemisphere.

For additional practice, turn to page 204.

For additional practice, turn to page 204.

Writing Application

Use adjectives that compare in a friendly letter that describes some places that you like to visit. Share your letter.

ADJECTIVES

SPECIAL FORMS OF ADJECTIVES

Some adjectives have special forms for comparing.

Positive	Comparative	Superlative
good	better	best
bad	worse	worst
much	more	most
little	less	least

Notice the difference between the adjectives *good* and *well*.

The poster looks <u>good</u> because I worked hard on it.

If I'm <u>well</u> enough, I'll take it to school tomorrow.

Think about why the forms of the underlined adjectives in the following sentences are correct.

Painting the faces was the <u>worst</u> part of the job.

I used <u>more</u> paint than my partner did.

In the previous lesson, you saw that *more* and *most* can be used to help adjectives compare. *Less* and *least* can be used in the same way.

likely	less likely	least likely
expensive	less expensive	least expensive

Exercise 30

Write the form of the *adjective* in parentheses that correctly completes each sentence.

1. We were all competing to see who could create the (good) poster about an ancient civilization.

2. The Great Wall of China wasn't a (bad) idea at all!

3. This poster is definitely (good) than last year's winner.

4. Ms. Martin is feeling (good) than she did yesterday, rather than (bad), so she'll judge the posters this afternoon.

5. This contest has been (much) fun than anything else I've done this month.

6. In fact, it may be the (good) activity of the year.

For additional practice, turn to page 204.

For additional practice, turn to page 204.

Writing Application

What might a visitor from an ancient culture say about life today? Write a dialogue between that person and yourself. Use adjectives that compare in your writing.

VERBS

VERB

A *verb* is a word that expresses action or being.

Garth talks constantly about the Middle Ages.
  expresses action

Those long-ago times are Garth's main interest.
  expresses being

ACTION VERB

An *action verb* tells what the subject does, did, or will do.

Many tourists visit castles in Europe.

How Garth enjoyed his visit there last summer!

He will return someday for another tour.

LINKING VERB

A *linking verb* connects the subject to a noun that renames the subject or to an adjective that describes it.

Ms. Taylor is Garth's helper.

She was a student in England at one time.

Garth's stories about castles have been wonderful.

The most common linking verb is *be*. Some forms of *be* are *am, is, are, was, were, has been,* and *have been.*

Exercise 31

Identify the *verb* or *verbs* in each sentence. Tell whether each verb is an *action* verb or a *linking* verb.

1. Castle builders worked hard at many tasks.
2. Carpenters and stonemasons were two kinds of workers.
3. Laborers cleared the site and leveled the ground.
4. Meanwhile, the landowner approved plans for the castle.
5. Blacksmiths repaired tools and weapons or forged new ones.
6. They were strong and skillful workers.

For additional practice, turn to pages 206–207.

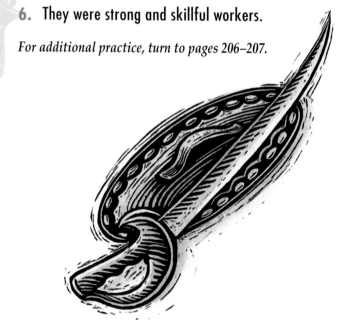

Writing Application

Would you want to live in a castle? Freewrite a response to that question. Then look at your response. What kinds of verbs did you use?

VERBS

MAIN VERB

A verb phrase is made up of two or more verbs. The *main verb* is the most important verb in a verb phrase.

My teacher *will tell* us about Peru.

Mr. Vargas *has been living* here for twelve years.

HELPING VERB

A *helping verb* helps the main verb express action or being. Forms of *be, have, do, can, will, may,* and *shall* can be used as helping verbs.

All of us *have drawn* maps of South America.

A main verb can have more than one helping verb.

We *should be starting* our special study next week.

Some of the verbs that can be used as helping verbs can also stand alone as main verbs.

We always *have* a good time in Mr. Vargas's class.

Sometimes other words appear between the helping verb and the main verb.

I *have* not *visited* South America.

Would you *make* such a long trip?

Exercise 32

Tell whether the underlined word in each sentence is a *main* verb or a *helping* verb.

1. We will take an imaginary trip through South America.
2. I have a map here for our reference.
3. The Amazon River has been flowing across Brazil for thousands of years.
4. I should have suspected that Brazil has a larger land area than the continental United States!

Exercise 33

Identify the verb phrase or phrases in each sentence. Then identify the main verb in each verb phrase.

5. We will pass through Bolivia on our way to Peru.
6. We must cross a mountain range.
7. Did you guess that Chile would be our next stop?
8. You have never seen such a long, narrow country.

For additional practice, turn to pages 208–209.

Writing Application

Gather ideas for a tour of a place that interests you. Then write a speech for a tour guide and share it with your classmates. Use at least four verb phrases in your speech.

149

VERBS

TRANSITIVE VERB

A *transitive verb* is an action verb that is followed by a noun or a pronoun that receives the action.

I *know* the story.

INTRANSITIVE VERB

Intransitive verbs include all linking verbs and any action verbs that do not take an object.

Greyfriars Bobby *was* a Skye terrier.

"Auld Jock" Gray *died*.

DIRECT OBJECT

The noun or pronoun that receives the action of the verb is the *direct object*. A direct object tells who or what receives the action.

Bobby loved his *master*.

INDIRECT OBJECT

An *indirect object* tells to whom or for whom the action of the verb is done.

Auld Jock showed the *dog* kindness.

Exercise 34

Identify each verb and tell whether it is *transitive* or *intransitive*. If it is transitive, identify its *direct object*. If there is also an *indirect object*, identify it.

1. Auld Jock's friends gave him a funeral service in Greyfriars Churchyard.

2. No one felt sadder than Bobby.

3. How Bobby loved the old shepherd!

4. The next day, the caretaker stopped and stared.

5. Bobby had found a home on top of the grave.

Exercise 35

Expand each sentence so that it will have an indirect object as well as a direct object.

6. Every day, an innkeeper and his wife brought food.

7. The people of Edinburgh told the story of Greyfriars Bobby.

8. When visitors came, Bobby gave a friendly wag of his tail.

For additional practice, turn to pages 210–211.

Writing Application

Use forms of the following verbs to write about a friend: give, offer, promise, buy, show, write, *and* tell. *Use direct and indirect objects. Share your writing.*

VERBS

PREDICATE NOMINATIVE

A *predicate nominative* is a noun or pronoun that follows a linking verb and renames the subject.

Lassie <u>has been</u> a *celebrity* for decades.

PREDICATE ADJECTIVE

A *predicate adjective* is an adjective that follows a linking verb and describes the subject.

Rin Tin Tin <u>was</u> *famous* in Hollywood, too.

LINKING/ACTION VERBS

Forms of *be* are the most common linking verbs. Other linking verbs include forms of *taste, look, smell, feel, appear, seem,* and *become.*

"Rinty" and Lassie <u>seem</u> *brave* in their films.

When audiences watched, they <u>felt</u> *good.*

Many of these other linking verbs can sometimes be used as action verbs. In these sentences, think about the differences in the verbs.

Rin Tin Tin *looked* fearless.

A twig snapped; "Rinty" *looked* in that direction.

Exercise 36

Tell whether each underlined word or group of words is a *predicate nominative* or a *predicate adjective*.

1. "Rinty" was a <u>puppy</u> when he came to America.
2. His owner and trainer was <u>Corporal Lee Duncan</u>.
3. "Rinty" seemed <u>clever</u> and <u>skillful</u> enough for dog shows.

Exercise 37

Identify the predicate nominatives and predicate adjectives in these sentences.

4. Rin Tin Tin became a star.
5. Did "Rinty" feel proud of his accomplishments?
6. Lassie appears brave and compassionate in her films.
7. She is still an inspiration today.

Exercise 38

Use each verb in two sentences. In the first sentence, use it as an action verb. In the second sentence, use it as a linking verb.

8. feel
9. taste
10. smell

For additional practice, turn to pages 212–213.

For additional practice, turn to pages 212–213.

Writing Application

Brainstorm ideas for a movie about a dog. Use at least two predicate nominatives and two predicate adjectives as you summarize the plot. Share your summary.

VERBS

TENSE

The *tense* of a verb shows time. Verb tenses change to indicate that events happen at different times. The simple tenses are the *present*, the *past*, and the *future*.

A verb in the *present tense* shows action that happens now or action that happens over and over. When the subject is *he*, *she*, *it*, or a singular noun, form the present tense of most verbs by adding *-s* or *-es*.

Dena *laughs* at Grandpa's silly story.

A verb in the *past tense* indicates action that took place in the past. Form the past tense of most verbs by adding *-ed* or *-d*.

Yesterday I *laughed* for five minutes without a rest.

Sometimes you need to change *y* to *i* before adding *-ed*. At other times, you must double the final consonant.

I *tried* it out on my sister.

She *slapped* her leg with laughter.

A verb in the *future tense* shows action that will happen in the future. Form the future tense of a verb by using the helping verb *will* with the main verb.

You and I *will laugh* about this tomorrow.

Exercise 39

Identify the verbs and verb phrases in these sentences. Tell whether each verb or verb phrase is in the *present,* the *past,* or the *future* tense.

1. My grandparents act in community theater productions.
2. Tomorrow they will practice for four hours.
3. I always memorize their lines and test them.
4. Last night they invited me to a rehearsal of their new play.
5. Ruth Rosen created and will direct *The Lines Punched Back.*

Exercise 40

Compose a sentence for each verb. Use the tense given in parentheses ( ).

6. guess (present)
7. answer (future)
8. study (past)
9. grin (past)

For additional practice, turn to pages 214–215.

For additional practice, turn to pages 214–215.

Writing Application

What's so funny? Write and share a story that makes you laugh. See whether you can identify present-tense, past-tense, and future-tense verbs in your writing.

▼
VERBS

PERFECT TENSE

There are three *perfect tenses*—*present perfect, past perfect,* and *future perfect.* The perfect tenses are made up of the past participle and a form of the helping verb *have.*

A verb in the *present perfect tense* shows action that started to happen sometime before now. The action may still be happening.

Mr. Lee *has arranged* a comedy show for us.

I *have seen* him talking to the principal about it.

A verb in the *past perfect tense* shows action that happened before a specific time in the past.

By dinner time, I *had planned* my entire act.

Amy told me that she already *had decided* on some jokes about school.

A verb in the *future perfect tense* shows action that will have happened before a specific time in the future.

By the time of our first rehearsal, Amy *will have mastered* her jokes.

I *will have selected* some new material before the day is over.

Exercise 41

Identify the verb phrases in these sentences. Tell whether each verb phrase is in the *present perfect*, the *past perfect*, or the *future perfect* tense.

1. Mr. Lee has started the rehearsal.

2. There had been a delay because a meeting had run long.

3. Amy, Bianca, Joey, and I have watched three skits already.

4. In a moment, we will have waited for a full hour.

Exercise 42

Complete each sentence, using the correct perfect tense of the verb in parentheses ( ).

5. Mr. Lee _____ _____ with us for a week now. (work)

6. Before these rehearsals, I _____ not _____ that he was so funny. (realize)

7. By next fall, he _____ _____ _____ here for ten years. (coach)

For additional practice, turn to pages 216–217.

For additional practice, turn to pages 216–217.

Writing Application

Brainstorm ideas for a funny dialogue between you and a friend. Use perfect tenses in the dialogue. Share your dialogue by performing it!

VERBS

PRINCIPAL PARTS

The four basic forms of a verb are its **principal parts.** These forms are the *infinitive,* the *present participle,* the *past,* and the *past participle.*

Infinitive	Present Participle	Past	Past Participle
(to) play	(is) playing	played	(has) played
(to) move	(is) moving	moved	(has) moved

Participles are forms used with helping verbs. The past and past participle of *regular verbs* are formed by adding **-ed** or **-d.**

IRREGULAR VERB

The past and past participle forms of *irregular verbs* are not formed by adding *-ed* or *-d.*

Infinitive	Past	Past Participle
(to) fly	flew	(has, have, had) flown
(to) grow	grew	(has, have, had) grown
(to) wear	wore	(has, have, had) worn
(to) begin	began	(has, have, had) begun
(to) drink	drank	(has, have, had) drunk
(to) bring	brought	(has, have, had) brought
(to) catch	caught	(has, have, had) caught

Exercise 43

Complete each sentence, using the correct form of the verb in parentheses ( ).

1. Have you ever _____ through a straw? (drink)

2. Martin Stone _____ out this invention in 1888. (bring)

3. Because the demand had _____ so great, he _____ using a machine to roll the straws. (grow; begin)

4. Any person who has _____ in an airplane, _____ a raincoat, or _____ a baseball in a mitt has benefited from modern inventions. (fly; wear; catch)

Exercise 44

Correct the error in each sentence.

5. Orville Wright first flyed an airplane in 1903.

6. Pete has drank carbonated water, an English invention.

7. Since 1922, car radios have brung drivers the news.

For additional practice, turn to pages 218–219.

For additional practice, turn to pages 218–219.

Writing Application

List as many verbs as you can in one minute. Decide which verbs are irregular. Use the irregular verbs to write a paragraph on a topic of your choice.

ADVERBS

ADVERB

An *adverb* modifies, or describes, a verb, an adjective, or another adverb. An adverb tells *how, when, where,* or *to what extent.* Many adverbs end in *-ly.*

Our skates moved *effortlessly.*
> *tells* how

The ice is glistening *now.*
> *tells* when

The canals are frozen *there.*
> *tells* where

The air was *very* dry.
> *tells* to what extent

Exercise 45

Identify the *adverb* that describes each underlined word. Then tell whether the adverb tells *how, when, where,* or *to what extent.*

1. Hans <u>dressed</u> warmly.
2. He <u>walked</u> outside and headed toward the canal.
3. He <u>waved</u> happily to his friends.
4. The air was quite <u>cold</u>.
5. Many people <u>skated</u> tonight.

For additional practice, turn to pages 220–221.

Looking at Language

I am from Haiti, a country on the island of Hispaniola. The other country on the island is the Dominican Republic. Hispaniola is in the Caribbean Sea, near the United States.

The official language of Haiti is French, but most people speak Creole. Creole is similar in some ways to French, but it is also very different. Many Creole speakers can understand French, but it is harder for French speakers to understand Creole.

One big difference between Creole and English is in forming verbs. In Creole, we use prefixes instead of "helping verbs." For example, to show future tense, we would not add the helping verb *will*; we would add the prefix *a-*, *va-*, or *ava-*. It looks like this:

We will arrive.	Nou a-rivé.
You will call.	Ou a-rélé.
He will stop.	Li va-rété.

ADVERBS

COMPARING WITH ADVERBS

Adverbs can be used to compare two or more actions. The *positive form* of an adverb is used when no comparison is being made.

The sun will set early.

Ice formed quickly on the windshield.

The *comparative form* is used to compare two actions. Form the comparative of most short adverbs by adding *-er* to the positive form.

Sunset comes earlier in the winter than in the summer.

With other adverbs, use more or less.

Weather changes more quickly in winter than in fall.

The *superlative form* is used to compare three or more actions. Form the superlative of most short adverbs by adding *-est* to the positive form.

Sunset comes earliest of all at the winter solstice.

With other adverbs, use most or least.

Weather changes most quickly with an east wind.

Well and *badly* have special forms for comparison.

Positive	Comparative	Superlative
well	better	best
badly	worse	worst

Exercise 46

Name the form of the adverb in parentheses that correctly completes each sentence.

1. **Ice melts (fast) on sunny days than on cloudy ones.**
2. **Snow comes (frequently) of all when the wind is from the north or the northwest.**
3. **The first snow comes (often) in November than in October.**

NEGATIVES

Negatives are words that mean "no." The words *no, not, never, nowhere, nothing, nobody, no one, neither, scarcely,* and *barely* are common negatives. Use only one negative in a sentence.

CORRECT: ***No one*** **should ever drive on ice.**

INCORRECT: ***No one*** **should** ***never*** **drive on ice.**

Exercise 47

Name the word in parentheses that correctly completes each sentence. Avoid double negatives.

4. **My friend Vince hadn't (ever, never) been to the Winter Carnival before.**
5. **He didn't have (no, any) idea that ice sculptures could be so large.**

For additional practice, turn to pages 222–223.

Writing Application

Brainstorm ideas for a description of a winter scene. Use adverbs to make your writing lively. Share your description.

PREPOSITIONS

PREPOSITION

A *preposition* shows the relationship of a noun or pronoun to another word in the sentence.

I walked <u>along</u> the beach.

Common Prepositions

about	before	for	of	to
along	behind	from	off	under
among	in	on	until	between
beneath	at	by	into	over
with	during	through		

OBJECT OF THE PREPOSITION

The noun or pronoun that follows a preposition is the *object of the preposition*.

The sands *of* the <u>beach</u> were white.

Exercise 48

The underlined word in each sentence is the object of a preposition. Identify the *preposition* for each object.

1. The boat took us into deep <u>water</u>.
2. We stopped in a certain <u>place</u>.
3. Everyone scanned the water through <u>binoculars</u>.
4. One of the passengers saw the tail of a <u>whale</u>.

PREPOSITIONAL PHRASE

A *prepositional phrase* is made up of a preposition, the object of the preposition, and all the words in between.

Who lives *in that house?*

It is supported *by wooden stilts.*

Exercise 49

Identify the *prepositional phrase* in each sentence. Name the preposition.

5. All heads turned to the right.
6. We could see eight whales in the group.
7. The whales showed curiosity about our ship.
8. We felt the excitement of the moment.
9. Most whales are among the endangered species.
10. Concern for the world's whales is growing.

For additional practice, turn to pages 224–225.

Writing Application

Write a narrative about an experience on the water. Use prepositional phrases in your writing. Share your narrative.

PREPOSITIONS

ADJECTIVE PHRASE

A prepositional phrase that modifies, or describes, a noun or a pronoun is an *adjective phrase.* An adjective phrase tells *what kind, which one,* or *how many.*

The killer whale is a species *of porpoise.*
>   *tells* what kind

That whale *with the unusual markings* is our favorite.
>   *tells* which one

A pod *of twenty whales* was sighted recently.
>   *tells* how many

Exercise 50

Identify the adjective phrase and the word it modifies.

1. The trainer of the porpoises waved her hand.
2. Many people in the crowd laughed.
3. The beginning of each show was the same.
4. The porpoises' leaps into the air were unbelievable.
5. A large pail held rewards for the performers.

ADVERB PHRASE

A prepositional phrase that modifies a verb, an adjective, or an adverb is an *adverb phrase.* An adverb phrase tells *how, when, where,* or *how often.*

The porpoises performed *with ease.*
   tells how

Shows begin *on the hour.*
   tells when

The porpoises swim *in a large tank.*
   tells where

They are rewarded *after each trick.*
   tells how often

Exercise 51

Identify each adverb phrase and the word it modifies.

6. **Whales are the largest mammals that live on the earth.**

7. **The whale you see in the picture is a blue whale.**

8. **Whales behave with great intelligence.**

9. **A whale must breathe air through its lungs.**

10. **Whales can dive for long periods.**

For additional practice, turn to pages 226–227.

For additional practice, turn to pages 226–227.

Writing Application

Write an informative essay about a sea animal. Use adjective and adverb phrases in your writing. Share your essay with classmates.

167

USAGE

Troublesome Words

Use *lie* when you mean "rest" or "recline."

I *lie* in the hammock after lunch.

Use *lay* when you mean "place something in a reclining position."

I *lay* the binoculars on the table.

Use *sit* when you mean "rest, as in a chair."

I *sit* at my desk to read.

Use *set* when you mean "put something in a certain place."

I *set* my book on a reading stand.

RISE, RAISE

Use *rise* when you mean "get up" or "move higher."

I *rise* from bed at 6:00 A.M.

Use *raise* when you mean "lift something up."

I *raise* the window shade.

Here are the principal parts of *lie, lay, sit, set, rise,* and *raise*:

Present	Past	Past Participle
lie(s)	lay	(have, has, had) lain
lay(s)	laid	(have, has, had) laid
sit(s)	sat	(have, has, had) sat
set(s)	set	(have, has, had) set
rise(s)	rose	(have, has, had) risen
raise(s)	raised	(have, has, had) raised

Exercise 52

Choose the word in parentheses that correctly completes each sentence.

1. Two whales (rise, raise) to the surface.
2. Do not (lie, lay) your case on the railing.
3. Will you (set, sit) here with me?
4. I like to (lay, lie) on the deck and watch for whales.
5. (Set, Sit) the chair over here.
6. One whale (rises, raises) its head out of the water.

For additional practice, turn to pages 228–229.

Standard vs. Nonstandard English

You usually change your language in some ways, depending on your audience. You often use slang when speaking to friends or classmates. Even the grammar of your sentences may be nonstandard.

In formal, public situations, however, your language should reflect standard English. Here are some things to remember when you speak or write standard English.

A subject and its verb should agree in number. Use the singular form of a verb with a singular subject. Use the plural form of a verb with a plural subject.

He *doesn't* like dogs.

> NOT:
> He <u>don't</u> like dogs.

Cats *don't* bark.

> NOT:
> Cats <u>doesn't</u> bark.

Sometimes a prepositional phrase comes between the subject and verb of a sentence. Be sure the verb agrees with the subject and not with the object of the preposition.

The colors in the painting *are* vivid.

> NOT:
> The colors in the painting <u>is</u> vivid.

Follow these rules for compound subjects joined by *or, either/or,* or *neither/nor.*

If both parts are plural, use a plural verb.

Either the boys or their parents *are driving* to the game.

If both parts are singular, use a singular verb.

Neither ivy nor moss *grows* here.

If one subject is singular and the other plural, the verb should agree with the subject closer to it.

Neither the cat nor the puppies *have* eaten yet.

Neither the puppies nor the cat *has* eaten yet.

I, ME

Use *I* as a subject pronoun.
Use *me* as an object pronoun.

Leo and *I* went fishing.

> *NOT:*
> **Leo and *me* went fishing.**

Between you and *me*, the water is too cold.

> *NOT:*
> **Between you and I, the water is too cold.**

When referring to yourself and someone else, refer to yourself last.

Sue sat by *Kim and me*.

> *NOT:*
> **Sue sat by me and Kim.**

CORRECT COMPARISONS

Use either *-er* or *more* to form the comparative, but not both.

That was the *prettier* of the two flowers.

> *NOT:*
> **That was the more prettier of the two flowers.**

Use either *-est* or *most* to form the superlative, but not both.

That star is the *brightest* one in the sky.

> *NOT:*
> **That star is the most brightest one in the sky.**

INCOMPLETE COMPARISONS

Use *other* or *else* when you compare one member of a group to the other members.

Rhode Island is smaller than *any other* state.

> *NOT:*
> **Rhode Island is smaller than any state.**

Susan is a better swimmer than *anyone else* in her class.

> *NOT:*
> **Susan is a better swimmer than anyone in her class.**

COMMA

Use a comma after a word or phrase that introduces a sentence.

Yes, there are many examples of bravery in that story.

In my opinion, the last chapter contains the most surprising tale of all.

Use a comma to set off the name of a person who is spoken to directly in a sentence.

Dan, it takes courage to stand up for your rights.

Tell me what you said, *Marie.*

Exercise 53

Add commas where they are needed.

1. Yes courage shows in many ways.

2. By the way did you decide to write a letter to the editor of the paper Karen?

3. To my way of thinking people should join together to fight for a cause.

4. Noah do your grandparents still volunteer?

COMMA

Use commas to set off words or phrases that interrupt a sentence, such as *for example, however,* or *in fact.*

This plane, *for example,* flies nonstop to Chicago.

An *appositive* is a noun or noun phrase that identifies or renames the word or words that precede it. Use commas to set off an appositive from the rest of the sentence.

Our steward, *James Moreno,* speaks three languages.

His home is in Rome, *the capital of Italy.*

Use a comma after each item except the last one in a series of three or more items.

He can converse in *French, Italian,* or *English.*

Exercise 54
Add commas where they are needed.

5. **Many people were traveling to Dallas Phoenix and Los Angeles.**

6. **The weather was in my opinion getting worse.**

7. **The pilot Captain Singrossi said to fasten our seat belts.**

8. **The pilot copilot and navigator flew us through the storm safely.**

For additional practice, turn to pages 230–231.

Writing Application

Write a narrative about someone who showed courage. Use commas in your writing. Share your narrative.

PUNCTUATION

Use quotation marks before and after a direct quotation.

"The truth is powerful and will prevail," said Sojourner Truth.

If a quotation is interrupted by other words, place quotation marks around the quoted words only.

"Give me liberty," Patrick Henry cried, "or give me death!"

Place a comma or a period inside closing quotation marks.

"I have read those words before," said Ben.

Place a question mark or an exclamation point inside closing quotation marks if the quotation itself is a question or an exclamation.

"Haven't you ever heard of Sojourner Truth or Patrick Henry?" asked Marcia.

Exercise 55

Add quotation marks where they are needed.

1. Queen Elizabeth I ruled a great empire, Marcia said.

2. She told her critics, I have the heart and stomach of a king.

3. Who else had a great impact on a country? asked Terri.

4. Well, Ben remarked, Mohandas Gandhi inspired a nonviolent revolution in India.

5. Nonviolence is not a garment, he wrote, to be put on and off at will.

6. Gandhi's words inspired Martin Luther King! Terri added.

For additional practice, turn to pages 232–233.

For additional practice, turn to pages 232–233.

Writing Application

Write a story about a leader you admire. Use dialogue in your writing. Share your story.

MECHANICS

TITLES

TITLES

Capitalize the first word, the last word, and all the important words in a title.

Place quotation marks around the titles of short works, such as poems, short stories, chapters, articles, and songs.

"From a Distance"   "To Make a Prairie"

"Building a Bird Feeder"   "The Listeners"

Underline the titles of books, plays, magazines, newspapers, television shows, and movies.

The Secret Garden   Los Angeles Times

60 Minutes   Pinocchio

Exercise 56
Capitalize and punctuate titles correctly.

1. Where is last week's issue of time?

2. Have you read John Steinbeck's book travels with charley?

3. I just found that article, welcome to pittsburgh.

4. Have you seen the movie beauty and the beast?

5. My family enjoys watching Monday night football.

For additional practice, turn to pages 234–235.

ABBREVIATIONS

Use a period after most abbreviations.

in. (inches)   **ft. (feet)**

Capitalize abbreviations that stand for proper nouns.

Ave. (Avenue)   **Oct. (October)**

You do not need to use periods when writing postal abbreviations of the fifty states or the abbreviations of some large organizations.

NH (New Hampshire)   **OH (Ohio)**
NATO (North Atlantic Treaty Organization)

You don't need to use periods with certain measurements.

cm (centimeter)   **km (kilometer)**

Exercise 57

Write the abbreviation of each item. Use a dictionary if necessary.

6. Lake Shore Drive
7. millimeter
8. New York
9. Saturday

For additional practice, turn to pages 236–237.

Writing Application

Write a letter to ask for travel information. Use titles and abbreviations in your letter. Share your letter.

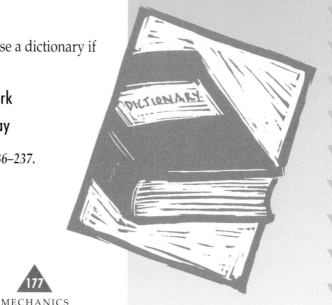

$A\ B\ C\ D\ E\ F\ G\ H\ I$

$J\ K\ L\ M\ N\ O\ P\ Q\ R$

$S\ T\ U\ V\ W\ X\ Y\ Z$

$a\ b\ c\ d\ e\ f\ g\ h\ i$

$j\ k\ l\ m\ n\ o\ p\ q\ r$

$s\ t\ u\ v\ w\ x\ y\ z$

$A\ B\ C\ D\ E\ F\ G\ H\ I$

$J\ K\ L\ M\ N\ O\ P\ Q\ R$

$S\ T\ U\ V\ W\ X\ Y\ Z$

$a\ b\ c\ d\ e\ f\ g\ h\ i$

$j\ k\ l\ m\ n\ o\ p\ q\ r$

$s\ t\ u\ v\ w\ x\ y\ z$

ADDITIONAL PRACTICE

Sentences 180

Nouns 194

Pronouns 198

Adjectives 202

Verbs 206

Adverbs 220

Negatives 223

Prepositions 224

Troublesome Words 228

Punctuation 230

Titles 234

Abbreviations 236

SENTENCES

A. Tell whether each group of words is a *sentence* or *not a sentence.*

Example:
A light danced in the sky.

Sentence

1. Moved rapidly.
2. It hovered quite close to the ground.
3. Making no noise at all.
4. We heard nothing.
5. The bottom of the object was lit brightly.
6. The object flew straight up and away.

B. Tell whether each sentence is *declarative* or *interrogative.* Then write the sentence correctly.

Example:
What is the shape of the object

Interrogative—What is the shape of the object?

7. There have been many reports of UFOs
8. Have you ever had such an experience
9. No, I haven't
10. I have read some of the reports, though
11. Has anyone seen the inside of a flying saucer

12. What did it look like

13. Were there instrument panels

14. There are no pictures available

15. One person described her experience

16. Was it printed in any magazine

C. Tell whether each sentence is *exclamatory* or *imperative*. Then write the sentence correctly.

Example:
What an amazing photograph that is

   Exclamatory—What an amazing photograph that is!

17. Look carefully at that photograph

18. What an unusual background it has

19. Observe the shape of the object

20. What a sweeping view of the sky this is

21. Give me that magnifying glass

22. How amazing the new technology is

23. Imagine yourself on a journey to a faraway planet

24. Describe your feelings

25. How lonely space must be

COMPLETE AND SIMPLE SUBJECTS

On your paper, make two columns. In the first column, write the *complete subject* of each sentence. In the second column, write the *simple subject* of each sentence.

Example:

Several members of the crew were sewing costumes.

Complete Subject	Simple Subject
Several members	*members*
of the crew	

1. Ann was working in the costume room.
2. Many costumes were still unfinished.
3. Other outfits needed alterations.
4. Four students joined the costume crew.
5. A new costume was needed right away.
6. The velvet fabric was a challenge to cut.
7. Ann cut the cloth according to the pattern.
8. The pieces of velvet fit together well.

9. A number of students were building sets.

10. The director of the play entered the costume room.

11. His name was Mr. Frank Farwell.

12. A full script of the play was in his hand.

13. He hurried over to Ann.

14. The girl with the leading role had become ill.

15. Ann had also auditioned for the part.

16. She had almost won the role.

17. Mr. Farwell had chosen Ann as the replacement.

18. The number of lines in Ann's role was large.

19. Ann's brother helped her with her lines.

20. Only one week of rehearsals remained.

21. The day of the last dress rehearsal finally arrived.

22. The rehearsal lasted a long time.

23. The members of the cast were nervous on opening night.

24. The big maroon curtain opened.

25. Ann's friends congratulated her on her success.

COMPLETE AND SIMPLE PREDICATES

On your paper, make two columns. In the first column, write the *complete predicate* of each sentence. In the second column, write the *simple predicate* of each sentence.

Example:

Ralph spaded the earth vigorously.

Complete Predicate	Simple Predicate
spaded the earth vigorously	spaded

1. He broke large lumps of earth into smaller ones.
2. He raked the surface of the soil.
3. Ralph's father laid plants on the ground.
4. The two gardeners dug a separate hole for each plant.
5. Ralph heaped new soil around the roots of the plants.
6. A hose lay nearby on the walkway.
7. Ralph's sister Liz watered the plants generously.
8. Fertilizer would help the plants' growth.

9. Ralph watered the plants every other day.

10. He also pulled weeds from the garden.

11. Green leaves sprouted soon on all the plants.

12. The stalks grew taller and taller.

13. All of Ralph's plants were growing well.

14. One healthy plant was smaller than the others.

15. That plant needed special care.

16. Ralph gave the little plant daily attention.

17. The other plants dwarfed the small one.

18. Ralph's father called the little plant the "runt" of the garden.

19. The little plant looked healthy.

20. None of the plants had produced any flowers.

21. Some plants would not bloom at all.

22. Ralph went out to the garden early one morning.

23. He inspected each plant.

24. Ralph called to the other members of the family.

25. The littlest plant of all had three lovely flowers!

COMPOUND SUBJECTS AND PREDICATES

Tell whether each sentence has a *compound subject* or a *compound predicate*. Then write the simple subjects in each compound subject and the simple predicates in each compound predicate.

Example:

Felicia opened the back door of the house and sat on the back steps.

> *Compound predicate—opened, sat*

1. Felicia and Alfio were unhappy.

2. Alfio came out of the house and joined Felicia.

3. The young girl and her twin brother would have a birthday soon.

4. They enjoyed life on the farm but were somewhat lonely.

5. Their mother and father had said nothing about the twins' birthday.

6. Alfio and Felicia had not expressed anything directly to their parents.

7. The twins' parents understood the problem and had discussed it.

8. The children's friends lived several miles away and rarely visited.

9. Felicia's parents sometimes talked with each other but kept their voices soft.

10. Felicia and Alfio woke up early on the morning of their birthday.

11. They rushed down the stairs and ran into the kitchen.

12. Mother was fixing breakfast and wished them a happy birthday.

13. The two children ate and then dressed.

14. Father came into the house but said nothing.

15. Then he took them outside and walked them to the barn.

16. Mother and father smiled at each other.

17. Father went into the barn and finally emerged with a young llama.

18. The llama was their birthday present and soon became everyone's favorite pet.

SIMPLE AND COMPOUND SENTENCES

Identify each sentence as a *simple sentence* or a *compound sentence*.

Example:
Llamas do not look like camels, but they are related to them.

Compound sentence

1. A llama is not a wild animal.

2. Llamas are quite gentle, and people often make pets of them.

3. The llama is native to South America.

4. Herds of llamas are kept by the native people of the mountains of Peru and Bolivia.

5. Llamas climb easily over rocky terrain and make good pack animals in the mountains.

6. A llama has two toes on each foot, and this physical trait gives it unusual climbing ability.

7. They have adapted to places between 10,000 and 17,000 feet above sea level.

8. A llama is not carnivorous and prefers grasses and leaves as food.

9. A llama has a cleft, or divided, upper lip, and it can nibble at all sorts of things easily.

10. These animals are tamer than domesticated farm animals.

11. They enjoy humans as company, and they are quite affectionate.

12. They have no natural defensive feature such as horns.

13. An angry llama will pull its ears back and spit.

14. Ruth Janette Ruck has a pet llama and has written a book about her experience.

15. The book is entertaining and informative, and interested people should read it.

16. Some experts on llamas do not have all their facts correct.

17. Ruck talked to one expert, and he told her something interesting.

18. The llama lacks speech organs and is mute.

19. Ruck herself discovered otherwise.

20. Llamas emit a humming sound, and you can hear it.

CLAUSES AND PHRASES

A. On your paper, make two columns. In the first column, list the underlined *phrases* from these sentences. In the second column, list the underlined *clauses*.

Example:
Frank stared <u>at the dirty walls</u> <u>as he stirred the paint.</u>

Phrase	*Clause*
at the dirty walls	*as he stirred the paint*

1. <u>Before he could paint them</u>, he had to wash the walls <u>of the dining room</u>.

2. Frank filled a bucket <u>with washing compound and water</u>.

3. Frank scrubbed hard <u>for two hours</u>, and at last the walls were free of dirt.

4. <u>When Frank finished</u>, he looked <u>at each wall</u>.

5. <u>Because the paint on one wall was thin</u>, Frank noticed something <u>beneath the surface</u>.

6. <u>With a scraper</u>, he peeled some paint <u>from one part of the wall</u>.

7. <u>A painting was revealed</u>; perhaps it was an old mural.

8. <u>After he called his father</u>, Frank scraped more paint <u>from the bottom of the wall</u>.

9. Frank continued <u>with the difficult job</u> <u>until all the paint had been scraped away</u>.

B. Tell whether the underlined group of words in each sentence is an *independent clause* or a *dependent clause*. If it is a dependent clause, identify the *subordinating conjunction* that connects it with the rest of the sentence.

Example:
All artists need inspiration for their work, and many of them gain such inspiration from the culture of their native land.

Independent clause

10. Diego Rivera was one of the greatest painters and muralists of Mexico.

11. Because he loved Mexico, his works often portray the culture and history of that country.

12. One of his paintings reflects the time before the Spanish conquered Mexico.

13. That painting shows the Zapotec Indians making gold jewelry.

14. Although Rivera did some of his most famous murals in Mexico City, several of his works were painted in the United States.

15. If you want to see one of Rivera's best works, visit the Detroit Institute of Arts.

COMPLEX SENTENCES

Tell whether each sentence is a *simple sentence,* a *compound sentence,* or a *complex sentence.*

Example:
Although no one is sure why, the number of salmon in the Pacific Northwest has decreased alarmingly.

Complex sentence

1. The salmon is perhaps the most endangered animal of the 1990s.

2. Logging caused a problem for the spotted owl, but the causes of the salmon problem are more complex.

3. Because a number of species of salmon are threatened, solutions will cost a great deal.

4. Where salmon spawn each year in the upper Columbia River Basin, the fish used to number anywhere from 10 million to 16 million.

5. That number is now down to about 2,500,000, and it may decrease further.

6. As some scientists calculate, perhaps nineteen types of salmon may already be extinct.

7. More than one-third of the entire habitat of the salmon has been destroyed.

8. The chinook salmon is a greatly endangered species, but the sockeye and the coho are also in trouble.

9. Another endangered fish is the steelhead trout.

10. Irrigation runoff water contains dangerous chemicals, and dams have reduced the water flow to rivers.

11. These two factors have damaged the rivers of the Northwest, but overfishing and building developments have also contributed.

12. Because dams block the water flow, the young salmon are not carried out to sea on strong currents of fresh water.

13. Even more fish have died because of a seven-year drought.

14. Fish born in man-made hatcheries do not swim upstream well since they do not have the energy of wild salmon.

15. Emergency rulings from the government may be necessary before real help for the salmon is possible.

ADDITIONAL PRACTICE

COMMON AND PROPER NOUNS

On your paper, make two columns. In the first column, list the *common nouns* in each sentence. In the second column, list the *proper nouns.*

Example:
Claude Monet first exhibited his paintings in Paris.

Common Nouns	*Proper Nouns*
paintings	*Claude Monet*
	Paris

1. Monet was the first painter of the school of painting called Impressionism.

2. The name of this new style came from a painting by Monet called *Impression: Sunrise.*

3. The movement began in nineteenth-century France.

4. Monet was joined by thirty-nine other artists.

5. Those painters included Pierre-Auguste Renoir, Edgar Degas, and Paul Cézanne.

6. The first exhibit of paintings by this group was in Paris in April 1874.

7. The Impressionists wanted to capture on canvas how the eye saw light.

8. These painters were concerned with the way objects reflect light.

9. Monet often painted from a boat on the Seine River.

10. Monet died on December 5, 1926.

SINGULAR AND PLURAL NOUNS

On your paper, make two columns. Label one *Singular* and the other *Plural.* Write each noun in the correct column. Then write the other form.

Example:
baby

Singular	*Plural*
baby	*babies*

1. hero
2. ox
3. blueberries
4. women
5. blush
6. mouth
7. reef
8. canary
9. glitches
10. umbrellas
11. wells
12. vase
13. mosses

14. lance
15. mass
16. patch
17. video
18. mouse
19. gulch
20. cello
21. wishes
22. zipper
23. flash
24. cities
25. puppy

POSSESSIVE NOUNS

A. Identify which groups of words in these sentences you could replace with *possessive nouns*. Then rewrite each sentence, using a possessive noun.

Example:
The first mathematicians of the ancient world were the Egyptians in Africa.

The ancient world's first mathematicians were the Egyptians in Africa.

1. The knowledge of mathematics and science of the ancient Egyptians was put to practical use.

2. The computation system of the Egyptians was used to find areas and volumes.

3. The standard unit of length of the surveyors was the *cubit*, the length of the forearm of a person.

4. The skill of the mathematicians in geometry was used in the construction of the pyramids.

5. The knowledge of the Egyptians of astronomy was also quite remarkable.

6. The observations of the astronomers led them to distinguish the stars from the planets.

7. Alexandria, Egypt, was the home of the most famous library of the ancient world.

8. The scroll collection of the Alexandrian Library was the largest of the ancient world.

B. Tell the *singular possessive* form of each noun.

Example:
week

week's

9. country
10. thief
11. Robert Frost
12. sculptor
13. minute
14. weaver

15. Samuel Clemens
16. wolf
17. nurse
18. King Henry
19. moment
20. secretary

C. Tell the *plural possessive* form of each noun.

Example:
women

women's

21. masters
22. workers
23. hours
24. oxen
25. spies
26. buffaloes

27. surgeons
28. (the) Toronto Blue Jays
29. sheep
30. secretaries

PRONOUNS

A. List the *personal pronouns* in these sentences. Tell the number and gender of each one.

Example:
When Christopher Columbus died in 1506, he was an unhappy man.

> *he; singular, masculine*

1. Columbus explored the islands he had found in the West Indies.

2. They were referred to as "the New World."

3. Queen Isabella gave her support to the journey.

4. Columbus was a great seaman, but his skills as a colonizer were poor.

5. He left a group of men at Hispaniola, but all of them were killed.

B. Identify each pronoun in the following sentences. Tell whether the pronoun is a *subject, object,* or *reflexive pronoun.*

Example:
Monica did not injure herself.

> *herself; reflexive*

6. Monica told herself that she must drive slowly.

7. Monica's younger sister and brother were with her.

8. Brother Bob said that he was hungry.

9. The children amused themselves by singing.

10. Cars pulled off the highway because it was icy.

11. Monica drove slowly, but she still lost control.

12. For a moment she found herself helpless.

13. Then she maneuvered the car and stopped it.

C. Tell the *antecedent* of each underlined pronoun.

Example:

Julia Ward Howe is remembered for the words she wrote for "The Battle Hymn of the Republic."

Julia Ward Howe

14. "John Brown's Body" was a popular song with Union soldiers as they marched in the Civil War.

15. Howe wrote her words to be sung to that melody.

16. Howe's song was published in a magazine, but she was not named as the author.

17. Many famous poets voiced their praise for the lyrics.

18. Her words remained popular with soldiers.

19. They sang them during World War I.

POSSESSIVE PRONOUNS

Write the *possessive pronoun* that is needed to complete each sentence.

Example:
Residents of St. Petersburg, Russia, are proud of _____ city.

  their

1. We traveled to St. Petersburg to visit _____ friends.

2. Boris took us to see some of the most beautiful sights in _____ native city.

3. I made sure I had brought _____ camera along.

4. Marie and I, together with _____ friends, took a boat down the canals of the city.

5. Boris pointed out palaces where some of Russia's great rulers had made _____ homes.

6. At night the sun still sheds _____ light on the city.

7. On nights at home, Russians love to make tea; it is _____ favorite beverage.

8. Tea and apple cake is a favorite late-night snack of _____.

9. St. Petersburg is full of flea markets where merchants show off _____ wares.

10. The traders set up _____ stalls along Nevsky Prospekt.

11. Marie invited us on a trip to one of _____ favorite places, the Kirov Islands.

12. This place has a charm all _____ own.

13. During World War II, the citizens of St. Petersburg endured a 900-day siege of _____ city by the Germans.

14. We saw a man with a ribbon on _____ coat, showing that he was a veteran of that siege.

15. People who suffered through that period wear _____ ribbons proudly.

16. Snow, ice, hunger, and disease took _____ toll among the brave residents of St. Petersburg.

17. _____ name at the time was Leningrad, in honor of Lenin, a leader of the revolution of 1917.

A D J E C T I V E S   A N D   A R T I C L E S

A. On your paper, make two columns. In the first column, list the *adjectives* and *articles* in each sentence. In the second column, tell the word that each adjective or article describes.

Example:
Cheetahs are large cats.

Adjective/Article	Word Described
large	cats

1. Cheetahs live on the grassy plains of Africa.

2. An adult cheetah can run at a top speed of 70 miles per hour.

3. Cheetahs live on the broad grasslands of the Serengeti.

4. They are found in various parts of India as well as in Africa.

5. The cheetah has a slender body.

6. The long legs of a cheetah cover ground quickly.

7. The coat is brownish yellow with black spots.

8. The hair on the underbelly is white.

9. The lordly lion is a daytime predator, but the cheetah is a nocturnal hunter.

10. The large cats are magnificent creatures.

B. List the *proper adjectives* in these sentences.

Example:
These Egyptian mummies are quite old.

> *Egyptian*

11. The Alexandrian library held the largest collection of scrolls in the ancient world.
12. Alexandria was the center of Mediterranean culture.
13. The Arabs moved the Egyptian capital from Alexandria to Cairo in the seventh century A.D.
14. Alexandria became part of the Turkish Empire.
15. The city was an important naval base for British ships during both world wars.

C. Rewrite each sentence using the *demonstrative adjective* correctly.

Example:
Where is Madagascar on these map?

> *Where is Madagascar on this map?*

16. Those island is off the coast of Mozambique.
17. This lemurs make their home on Madagascar.
18. That animals can be found nowhere else.
19. Those rain forest is being cut down.
20. These destruction is ruining many habitats.

COMPARING WITH ADJECTIVES: POSITIVE, COMPARATIVE, AND SUPERLATIVE FORMS

A. Give the *comparative* and *superlative* forms of these adjectives.

Example:
hot

hotter, hottest

1. salty
2. odd
3. beautiful
4. dim
5. mischievous

6. brave
7. muddy
8. confident
9. simple
10. rosy

B. Write the form of the adjective in parentheses ( ) that correctly completes the sentence.

Example:
Which cruise ship has the (low) cost of all?

lowest

11. Which cruise takes the (long) time of all?
12. Is this ship (long) than that one?
13. Which of the cruises has the (tasty) food?
14. A (small) ship might be more fun than a (large) one.

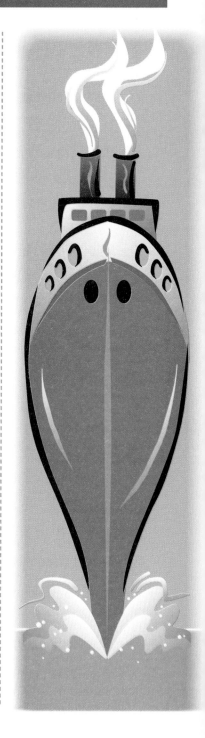

15. Once, only the (wealthy) people of all could afford cruises.

16. Now, prices are (cheap) and (affordable) than they once were.

17. Cruises are (popular) than ever before.

18. Ads for cruises in newspapers and on TV are (common) than they once were.

19. The cost for a luxury cruise is (great) than for any other.

20. Does this cruise have a (high) cost than that cruise?

C. Write the form of the adjective in parentheses ( ) that correctly completes the sentence.

Example:
The (good) thing to do on a trip is to travel light.
   best

21. Less baggage is (good) than (much) baggage.

22. Of these two brochures, this one is (bad).

23. There are (much) pictures than words.

24. I was sick on the first day, but now I feel (good).

25. The cruise with the (little) cost of all is to Aruba.

ACTION AND LINKING VERBS

On your paper, make two columns. In the first column, list the *verb* or verbs in each sentence. In the second column, tell whether the verb is an *action* verb or a *linking* verb.

Example:
I remember the drive vividly.

Verb	Action/Linking
remember	action

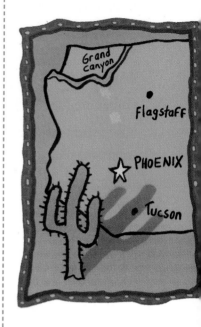

1. To those from warm climates, snow seems foreign.
2. We drove from Tucson to the Grand Canyon, in Arizona.
3. You literally go from one type of weather to the other.
4. The canyon is high above sea level.
5. Snow falls heavily there in winter.
6. In Tucson, temperatures are quite warm all year.
7. Arizona is definitely a world full of contrasts.

8. You see three different cultures everywhere.

9. The cultures are Anglo-American, Spanish, and Native American.

10. I recall the trip from Phoenix to Flagstaff.

11. I saw some of the most beautiful scenery.

12. We traveled from Prescott up to Sedona.

13. One scenic drive is the 16-mile road through Oak Creek Canyon.

14. The road ascends steadily to Flagstaff.

15. Strange things happen in the air at the Grand Canyon.

16. Sometimes you see the opposite side of the canyon.

17. At the same time, fog obscures the interior of the canyon.

18. At the bottom of the canyon flows the Colorado River.

19. There are many amazing sights nearby.

20. The Petrified Forest and the Painted Desert are memorable.

21. Petrified wood is wood that has turned to stone.

22. Guards protect petrified wood in the park from thieves.

23. Petrified wood has become a popular souvenir.

24. A meteor once hit near Winslow, Arizona.

25. It created Meteor Crater, which is 4,150 feet in diameter.

MAIN AND HELPING VERBS

A. Tell whether the underlined word in each sentence is a *main verb* or a *helping verb*.

Example:

The audience is <u>waiting</u> patiently.

Main verb

1. The tiny curtain slowly <u>opens</u>.
2. Two figures <u>are</u> dancing into view.
3. The figures are <u>called</u> puppets.
4. Puppets can be <u>made</u> out of cloth and wood.
5. Our puppet theater <u>gives</u> three shows a year.
6. Each show <u>is</u> performed for four weekends.
7. New plays are <u>rehearsed</u> carefully.
8. I <u>have</u> become a puppeteer with the company.
9. I <u>am</u> memorizing lines and movements.
10. The new play was <u>written</u> in Spanish and English.
11. Sometimes our lines are <u>spoken</u> in English.
12. Sometimes audiences <u>have</u> asked for Spanish.
13. All the puppeteers <u>can</u> speak both languages.

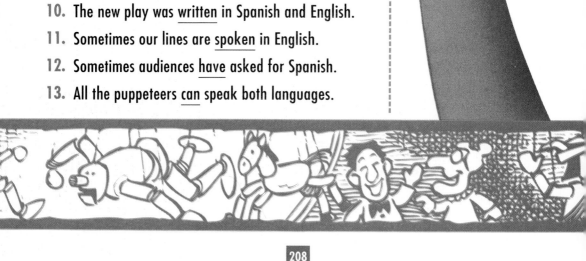

14. We have been <u>doing</u> this for several years.

15. <u>Do</u> the audiences enjoy the shows?

B. Identify the *verb phrase* in each sentence. Then identify the *main verb* in each verb phrase.

Example:
Puppets are worked by hand from underneath.

are worked; worked

16. The puppet's body is made from a piece of cloth.

17. The body is fitted over the puppeteer's hand.

18. A thumb and forefinger can become the puppet's arms.

19. Other fingers are used in head movements.

20. Jim Henson is credited with creating a special kind of hand puppet for television.

21. His puppets are called Muppets.

22. Workers must use two hands for movements.

23. One hand is employed for the puppet's facial expressions.

24. Fingers can create smiles or frowns.

25. The other hand may move the hand or body.

TRANSITIVE AND INTRANSITIVE VERBS/DIRECT AND INDIRECT OBJECTS

A. On your paper, make four columns. List each verb in the first column. Tell whether it is *transitive* or *intransitive* in the second column. If it is transitive, write its direct object in the third column. If there is also an indirect object, write it in the fourth column.

Example:

I gave the workers their money.

Verb	Type	Direct Object	Indirect Object
gave	*transitive*	*money*	*workers*

1. The workers had built a sturdy metal fence.
2. I inherited a cat from the former tenants.
3. Smith, the cat, sat quietly on the sofa.
4. I drove to the kennel for my two dogs, Jones and Koko.
5. The dogs would see Smith soon.
6. I offered the dogs treats.
7. I gave each dog a warning about politeness.
8. Then I entered the house with the two canines.
9. The cat bristled.
10. I gave the cat a hug.
11. The poodle, Koko, gave the cat a sniff.

12. Jones understood cats.

13. He sat quietly at a distance.

14. The cat surprised the dogs.

15. He gave each one a friendly kiss.

B. Expand each sentence so that it will have an indirect object as well as a direct object. Write the new sentences.

Example:

I brought treats.

I brought the animals treats.

16. When their guests arrived, the three pals gave a hearty welcome.

17. I sent holiday cards with pictures of the animals.

18. My friends asked questions about the first meeting.

19. A TV talk show host gave a spot on her program.

20. I told the facts.

21. An animal-food company sent boxes of free food.

22. A restaurant owner gave a free meal.

23. The animals brought a lot of public attention.

24. My neighbors bought new leashes.

25. The animals still give friendly greetings.

PREDICATE NOMINATIVES AND PREDICATE ADJECTIVES

A. Tell whether each underlined word or group of words is a *predicate nominative* or a *predicate adjective*.

Example:
A Halloween pumpkin is a jack-o'-lantern.

Predicate nominative

1. A pumpkin is really a squash.
2. In New England, "squash pie" is a favorite dessert.
3. The squash in the pie is pumpkin, of course.
4. Our family's pie maker is Uncle Oscar.
5. Oscar's pies are delicious.
6. As they come out of the oven, they look scrumptious.
7. Oscar's secret is the seasoning.
8. The pumpkin should not be too large.
9. Jack-o'-lanterns can be big or small.
10. A freshly baked pie is a delight to the eye.

B. Identify the *predicate nominatives* and *predicate adjectives* in these sentences.

Example:
That pumpkin looks strange.

strange; predicate adjective

11. It is quite heavy.
12. A pumpkin can become very large.
13. This one seems the largest.
14. It is the prizewinner.
15. At pumpkin time, the weather turns cold.
16. After the first frost, temperatures become mild again.
17. That warm period is called Indian summer.

C. Use each of these verbs in two sentences. In the first sentence, use the verb as an *action verb*. In the second sentence, use it as a *linking verb*.

18. turn
19. appear
20. feel

PRESENT, PAST, AND FUTURE TENSES

A. Identify the verbs or verb phrases in these sentences. Tell whether each verb is in the *present*, the *past*, or the *future tense*.

Example:
The Little League played a game today.

played; past

1. Teddy's team will bat first.
2. The visiting team always bats first.
3. Teddy's cousin Mary will pitch for his team.
4. In the last game, she played first base.
5. Sometimes players change positions.
6. The coach gives everyone a chance at each position.
7. The visiting team scored one run in the first inning.
8. Our team fields well.
9. Teddy missed the first two pitches.
10. The ball sailed toward right field.
11. Teddy's home run ties the game.
12. Mary pitched seven innings.
13. Will the coach replace her?
14. The crowd cheered her as she walked off the field.
15. Our team will celebrate its third victory.

B. Write a sentence for each verb. Use the tense given in parentheses ( ).

Example:
watch (past)

We watched the game closely.

16. shout (past)
17. surprise (future)
18. clap (present)
19. shrug (past)
20. use (future)
21. look (present)
22. ask (present)
23. wander (past)
24. explore (past)
25. attend (future)

PERFECT TENSES

A. Identify the verb phrases in these sentences. Tell whether each verb phrase is in the *present perfect,* the *past perfect,* or the *future perfect* tense.

Example:
Marla has purchased a new camera.

has purchased; present perfect

1. Marla has joined a camera club.
2. She has made photography her hobby.
3. The photo club had given her a prize.
4. By next month, Marla will have been a club member for three years.
5. The club has sponsored a contest every year for five years.
6. They have given more than fifty prizes so far.
7. By next year, they will have awarded more than sixty.
8. Marla had applied for club membership twice before.
9. Until this month, club members had needed a darkroom.
10. Members have applied part of their dues to the purchase of equipment.

B. Write each sentence using the correct perfect tense of the verb in parentheses ( ).

Example:
Your camera _____ repairs for some time. (need)

Your camera has needed repairs for some time.

11. I _____ a lot of film in the past two weeks. (use)

12. By the end of the month, I _____ more than $100 worth of film. (purchase)

13. Nila _____ many pictures of fall foliage this year. (snap)

14. She _____ pictures every year to magazines. (submit)

15. Recently, one magazine _____ her a job as a free-lance photographer. (promise)

16. Before that offer, she _____ her abilities. (doubt)

17. By next January, she _____ more than $5,000. (earn)

18. She _____ a new camera for herself. (purchase)

19. Nila _____ some of her techniques to me. (reveal)

20. Before I bought my new camera, I _____ only black-and-white film. (use)

P R I N C I P A L   P A R T S /
I R R E G U L A R   V E R B S

A. Write each sentence using the correct form of the verb or verbs in parentheses ( ).

Example:

We _____ to the circus last night. (go)

We went to the circus last night.

1. The circus _____ with a grand parade. (begin)

2. Every performer _____ a glittery costume. (wear)

3. I had _____ to the circus only once before. (be)

4. We had _____ refreshments before we _____ into the arena. (buy, go)

5. We like to _____ close to the top of the tent. (sit)

6. I could _____ the high-wire acts clearly. (see)

7. The acrobats _____ expertly through the air. (fly)

8. I had _____ there would _____ safety nets. (think, be)

9. Someone _____ the acrobat each time. (catch)

10. Have you ever _____ any acrobatic tricks? (do)

11. Our gym teacher has _____ us some tumbling skills. (teach)

12. I will never _____ those lessons. (forget)

13. I had not _____ the difficulty of such tricks. (understand)

14. We _____ the animals perform many feats. (see)

15. The work of the animal trainer _____ dangerous. (be)

B. Find the error or errors in each sentence. Write the sentence correctly.

Example:

One elephant hold a ball on the end of its trunk.

One elephant held a ball on the end of its trunk.

16. I have eat too many snacks.

17. Celia has came to the circus for five years.

18. Her aunt brung her this year.

19. Paolo has went only once before.

20. I had never seed a circus with three rings.

21. Paolo teared his shirt on a splinter.

22. I losed my hat in the crowd.

23. The clowns throwed candy into the crowd.

24. I catched two pieces.

25. When the acrobats flyed in the air, I nearly freezed with fear.

ADDITIONAL PRACTICE

ADVERBS

Identify the *adverb* that describes each underlined word or group of words. Then tell whether the adverb tells *how, when, where,* or *to what extent.*

Example:
The waves washed the shore gently.

gently; how

1. The sun shone down on the beach.
2. Children splashed noisily in the water.
3. Clouds scudded swiftly across the sky.
4. The serious surfers arrived first on the beach.
5. The largest crowds appeared later.
6. Lifeguards watched the swimmers carefully.
7. A strong undertow could be very dangerous.
8. One lifeguard warned a swimmer sternly.
9. Some swimmers seemed completely unaware of the danger.
10. Smart swimmers always observe the rules.
11. The children quickly built a castle in the sand.
12. A big wave washed the castle away.

13. The young architects soon <u>constructed</u> another.

14. A very <u>wide</u> moat surrounded the new building.

15. The sand grew quite <u>hot</u> under the blazing sun.

16. People quickly <u>disappeared</u> under wide umbrellas.

17. A cool breeze <u>floated</u> overhead.

18. People <u>applied</u> sun block generously.

19. Some bathers wisely <u>had brought</u> picnic lunches.

20. The wind suddenly <u>became</u> cool.

21. Dark clouds completely <u>hid</u> the sun.

22. Swimmers rapidly <u>packed</u> their gear.

23. Some swimmers <u>huddled</u> quietly under their umbrellas.

24. Lifeguards shouted very <u>loudly</u> to those in the water.

25. Few people <u>remained</u> there on the beach.

COMPARING WITH ADVERBS

A. Write the form of the adverb in parentheses ( ) that correctly completes the sentence.

Example:
Rain falls (heavily) in some regions than in others.

more heavily

1. In tropical climates, rainstorms occur (frequently) than in temperate zones.

2. Clouds fill with moisture (readily) over water than over land.

3. You can actually see the rain (easily) of all in places like Florida.

4. The wind direction shifts (noticeably) in the summer than in the winter.

5. In all its travels, the air soaks up moisture (rapidly) when it passes over the oceans.

B. Choose the word in parentheses ( ) that correctly completes the sentence. Avoid double negatives.

Example:
Don't (ever, never) cook rotten fish.

ever

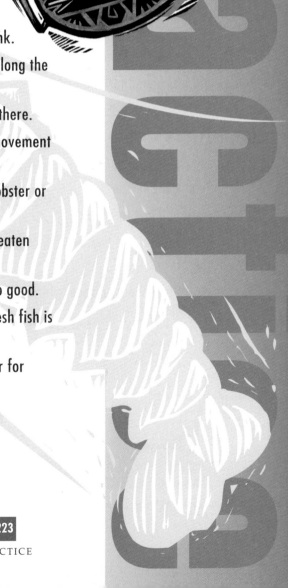

6. Haven't you (never, ever) eaten fish?

7. There isn't (no, any) tastier food, I think.

8. You won't (never, ever) find shellfish along the surface of the sea.

9. There is (no, any) way they can move there.

10. Shellfish haven't (any, no) means of movement except along the sea bottom.

11. Some people won't (ever, never) eat lobster or crab meat.

12. Marvin said that he had (ever, never) eaten mackerel before.

13. He says nothing (ever, never) tasted so good.

14. When you live near the sea, buying fresh fish is (no, any) problem at all.

15. There isn't (anywhere, nowhere) better for someone who likes fish.

PREPOSITIONS AND OBJECTS OF THE PREPOSITION

A. The underlined word in each sentence is the *object of a preposition*. Write the *preposition* for each object.

Example:

The ship steamed slowly down the river.

down

1. Many passengers leaned over the railing.
2. The ship was bound for England.
3. People waved to the passengers.
4. A few people walked down the gangplank.
5. The ship would soon be sailing into the Atlantic Ocean.
6. The trip would last for five days.
7. For many people, this had been their first sea voyage.
8. That must have been a pleasant form of travel.

PREPOSITIONAL PHRASES

B. Write the *prepositional phrase* or phrases in each sentence. Identify the preposition.

Example:
The Chinese were the greatest sailors in history.

in history; in

9. The rudder, the single mast, the square sail, and the compass were all invented by the Chinese.

10. Can you imagine steering a boat without a rudder?

11. Sailors have always been guided by the stars in clear weather.

12. The use of the compass made navigation in cloudy weather possible.

13. The compass was first mentioned in a book written in 1117.

14. The compass was actually invented in China at a much earlier date.

15. The time of this invention was the fourth century B.C.

ADJECTIVE PHRASES

A. Write the sentences. Underline the *adjective phrases*. Draw an arrow from the phrase to the word it modifies.

Example:
Three-fourths of the earth's surface is covered by water.

Three-fourths of the earth's surface is covered by water.

1. Two percent of that amount is frozen.
2. Rivers and lakes contain one percent of that water.
3. The oceans contain the rest of the water.
4. The four great oceans of the earth are the Atlantic, the Pacific, the Indian, and the Arctic.
5. The Pacific is the largest ocean on the earth.
6. The taste of ocean water is salty.
7. Dissolved salts make up four percent of ocean water.
8. That amount of salt makes ocean water really salty.
9. One mouthful of ocean water has more salt than a mouthful of potato chips.
10. Gulps of ocean water are quite unpleasant.

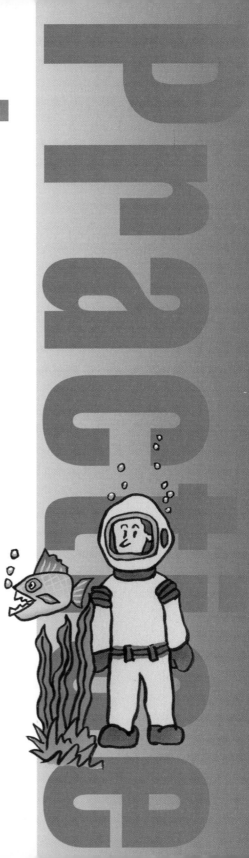

ADVERB PHRASES

B. Write the sentences. Underline the *adverb phrases*.
Draw an arrow from the phrase to the word it modifies.

Example:
Oceanographers work beneath the ocean's surface.

Oceanographers work beneath the ocean's surface.

11. They descend in small diving ships.

12. Water pressure would crush some ships in a moment.

13. Specially designed ships can descend to 4,000-foot depths.

14. These vessels are designed for quick maneuvers.

15. Some of these ships carry scientists to the ocean floor.

16. Scientists view sunken ships with robotic cameras.

17. These robots can be maneuvered by remote control.

18. Television cameras send pictures to the surface.

19. Where water is not so deep, scientists are protected with diving suits.

20. Scientists can also descend in special underwater vehicles.

TROUBLESOME WORDS

A. Choose the word in parentheses ( ) that correctly completes each sentence.

Example:
Tides (raise, rise) and fall each day.

rise

1. (Sit, Set) your beach bag on the car seat.
2. Soon we shall be (laying, lying) on the beach.
3. The temperature may (raise, rise) quite high today.
4. We should not (lay, lie) in the sun too long.
5. Let's (set, sit) down over there.
6. (Raise, Rise) your head so that I can put lotion on the back of your neck.
7. I'll (set, sit) the tube on the blanket.
8. We can (lie, lay) in the shade of those trees if we need to.
9. The sun (raised, rose) at 5:00 this morning.
10. It will not (set, sit) until early evening.

11. The whitecaps are (raising, rising) higher and higher.

12. Should we (lie, lay) down and let them roll over us?

13. I'd rather (set, sit) than (lie, lay) there.

14. I don't want to (raise, rise) my head and get a mouthful of salty water.

15. Well, then, let's (set, sit) in the shallow area.

16. Where did I (lie, lay) the water jug?

17. It's (laying, lying) right next to the picnic basket.

18. I (rose, raised) these tomatoes in my garden.

19. (Set, Sit) the salt and pepper shakers over here.

20. (Rise, Raise) yourself a little more, and I will brush the sand off your back.

21. I guess I (lay, lied) on the sand too long today.

22. Let's swim a bit and then (lay, lie) down again.

23. I can't tell if the tide is (raising, rising) or falling.

24. It's falling, because there's more beach to (set, sit) on now.

25. Oh, let's just (lie, lay) here and watch the waves.

PUNCTUATION: COMMAS WITH INTRODUCTORY WORDS AND DIRECT ADDRESS

A. Write each sentence, adding *commas* where they are needed.

Example:

Yes meadows are hard to find John.

Yes, meadows are hard to find, John.

1. Listen to me Sally.
2. Sally we are going to the Chicago Botanical Gardens today.
3. Well they have a new attraction.
4. No it's not a garden of exotic flowers.
5. Oh I thought I'd surprise you.
6. Okay it's a prairie garden.
7. The garden covers 15 acres Jed.
8. Yes humans have plowed up millions of acres of prairie for buildings.
9. No there are only about 2,300 acres of natural prairie left in Illinois now.
10. This man-made prairie is the botanists' gift to Illinois Sally.

COMMAS WITH INTERRUPTERS, APPOSITIVES, AND SERIES

B. Write each sentence, adding *commas* where they are needed.

Example

Roses paintbrush and clover are three plants you will find on the prairie.

Roses, paintbrush, and clover are three plants you will find on the prairie.

11. A prairie some people say is just a weed patch.

12. A prairie a kind of grassland is home to many kinds of plants and animals.

13. Animals feed on the leaves roots and stems of prairie plants.

14. Botanists according to a brochure transplanted 250,000 plants.

15. The total number of species in the garden I think is 250.

PUNCTUATION: DIALOGUE AND DIRECT QUOTATIONS

Write each sentence. Add *quotation marks* where they are needed.

Example:

New York has a new program, Nancy said, for student ticket buyers.

"New York has a new program," Nancy said, "for student ticket buyers."

1. Yes, replied Mrs. Bensen. It's called High Five. Student tickets cost only five dollars.
2. All you need to do is show your school identification card, said Ben.
3. That sounds like a wonderful idea, Sam said.
4. Mrs. Bensen said, Some tickets you can buy right at box offices.
5. Others you can get at special ticket locations, she added.
6. Nancy remarked, You can also get tickets to dance programs and symphony concerts.
7. What a great idea! exclaimed Ralph.

8. The full price of a theater ticket is not cheap, said Sam.

9. Productions of Shakespeare's plays are available all over the city, I believe, said Mrs. Bensen.

10. Broadway shows are not available yet, but off-Broadway shows are, said Nancy.

11. Say, said Ralph, why don't we try to get something like that right here?

12. Well, said Mrs. Bensen, the city does have a cultural affairs department.

13. Let's write them a letter, said Nancy.

14. How about church choirs? asked Nancy. They often give concerts.

15. Those are good suggestions, said Mrs. Bensen. Let's put them in our letter.

SHAKESPEARE

ADDITIONAL PRACTICE

TITLES

Write any *titles* in the following sentences correctly.

Example:
The magazine natural history is published by the American Museum of Natural History.

Natural History

1. One article listed in it is called our ecological past.

2. Did you see that movie about Dian Fossey called Gorillas in the Mist?

3. The planetarium has a holiday show called star of christmas.

4. Another museum tradition is what they call the origami holiday tree.

5. If you visit New York, try to see the phantom of the opera.

6. One show I'd enjoy seeing is guys and dolls.

7. It features the song luck be a lady tonight.

8. The musical cats is based on a book of poems by T. S. Eliot.

9. Eliot called his book old possum's book of practical cats.

10. One of the poems is called old deuteronomy.

11. Another poem is called macavity: the mystery cat.

12. The oldest cat of all sings the song memory.

13. A French play called cyrano de bergerac was turned into the musical cyrano.

14. The red shoes is based on a movie by the same name.

15. Will anyone ever write a musical based on the house at pooh corner?

ABBREVIATIONS

Write a correct *abbreviation* of each term. Use a
dictionary, if necessary.

Example:
Maine

 ME

1. **pound**
2. **ounce**
3. **foot**
4. **yard**
5. **kilometer**
6. **milligram**
7. **liter**
8. **cubic centimeter**

9. United States Military Academy

10. National Basketball Association

11. Michigan Boulevard

12. Rodeo Drive

13. Old Post Road

14. Fifth Avenue

15. National Collegiate Athletic Association

16. medical doctor

17. miles per hour

18. revolutions per minute

19. Fahrenheit

20. Celsius

STUDY SKILLS

Active Reading Strategies   240

Strategies for Reading Fiction   242

Strategies for Reading Nonfiction   244

Vocabulary Strategies   246

Listening and Speaking Strategies   248

Researching Information   250

The Library   252

Active Reading Strategies

Reading strategies enhance your understanding and appreciation of what you read.

You probably preview and set your purposes for reading automatically now, and don't even have to think about predicting. Just to refresh your memory, however, look at these useful reading strategies.

BEFORE READING

- **PREVIEW** Examine the cover, look at several pages, and read a paragraph here and there.

- **PREDICT WHAT THE BOOK WILL BE ABOUT** Making predictions will help you decide whether you want to read the book.

- **CHOOSE YOUR PURPOSE FOR READING** Ask yourself, "What do I want to learn from this material?"

DURING READING

- **CHECK YOUR PREDICTIONS** You may need to revise them as you read.

- **MONITOR YOUR OWN UNDERSTANDING** Occasionally stop and ask yourself if you are really understanding what you are reading. If not, reread or summarize what you've read so far.

- **RELATE TO YOUR OWN EXPERIENCE** As you read, think about whether the characters and their experiences are similar to anyone or anything in your own life.

- **VISUALIZE** Try to see in your mind the scenes the author has created.

- **LISTEN TO THE WORDS** This strategy is especially effective for reading fiction, plays, and poems. Does the dialogue sound real? Is the description so vivid that you feel you are there? Does that phrase or sentence put words together in a new way?

AFTER READING

- **SUMMARIZE** again. Remember the main ideas.

- **COMPARE** what you have read to what you knew earlier. Think about how your reading has changed your understanding.

- **EVALUATE** your reading. Think how you can use what you have learned.

Finally, remember that you are the one who knows best how to help yourself read better. Know *how* to use the strategies, and know *when* to use them.

STUDY SKILLS

Strategies for Reading Fiction

When you read fiction, your main purpose is often entertainment. But even when you are reading for pleasure, it is worthwhile to use strategies. Previewing, predicting, visualizing, and drawing conclusions — to name only a few — can help you get more out of your reading.

Follow the notes for the strategies one student used when reading *Island of the Blue Dolphins*.

*An Aleut ship...
an island...I wonder if
this story is set near
Alaska's Aleutian
Islands.*

Is the narrator a girl?

*This story must
be set in the past.*

from Island of the Blue Dolphins
by Scott O'Dell

I remember the day the Aleut ship came to our island. At first it seemed like a small shell afloat on the sea. Then it grew larger and was a gull with folded wings. At last in the rising sun it became what it really was—a red ship with two sails.

My brother and I had gone to the head of a canyon that winds down to a little harbor which is called Coral Cove. We had gone to gather roots that grow there in the spring.

My brother Ramo was only a little boy half my age, which was twelve. He was small for one who had lived so many suns and moons, but quick as a cricket. Also foolish as a cricket when he was excited. For this reason and because I wanted him to help me gather roots and not go running off, I said nothing about the shell I saw or the gull with folded wings.

I went on digging in the brush with my pointed stick as though nothing at all were happening on the sea. Even when I knew for sure that the gull was a ship with two red sails.

But Ramo's eyes missed little in the world. They were black like a lizard's and very large and, like the eyes of a lizard, could sometimes look sleepy. This was the time when they saw the most. This was the way they looked now. They were half-closed, like those of a lizard lying on a rock about to flick out its tongue to catch a fly.

Grateful acknowledgment is made to Houghton Mifflin Company for permission to reprint from *Island of the Blue Dolphins* by Scott O'Dell. Text copyright © 1960, renewed 1988 by Scott O'Dell.

Strategies for Reading Nonfiction

The information in nonfiction is often organized and made clear with headings, illustrations, and diagrams.

K – W – L

One strategy that can help you read nonfiction more effectively is **K–W–L**.

- **K** stands for "What I **K**now." Ask yourself what you already know about the topic. Then preview the selection.

- **W** means "What I **W**ant to Know." Think of questions based on the topic that you want to answer as you read.

- **L** is for "What I **L**earned." After you read, summarize what you have learned.

Before you read, make a K–W–L chart like the one below and fill in the first two columns. After you have finished reading, write your answers in the third column of the chart.

K – W – L Strategy

What I Know	What I Want to Know	What I Learned
Vietnam is a country in Southeast Asia. Some immigrants from Vietnam live in the United States.	What problems do the Vietnamese face? What are their families like?	

S Q 3 R

Another effective strategy for reading nonfiction is known as **SQ3R,** which stands for **S**urvey, **Q**uestion, **R**ead, **R**ecite, and **R**eview.

Survey

Preview the passage, paying special attention to titles, subtitles, and illustrations. Predict what the selection is likely to be about, and identify the topic.

Question

Use what you surveyed to think of questions you think the selection will answer.

Read

Keep the questions in mind as you read the selection. Revise your predictions to fit what you read.

Recite

Identify the main points of each section. This is one way to make sure you understand and remember.

Review

After you **Read** and **Recite**, **Review** by answering the **Questions** you asked at the beginning.

STUDY SKILLS

Vocabulary Strategies

Many English words are taken from other languages. Words with Greek and Latin origins became part of the English language centuries ago.

Sometimes you can figure out an unfamiliar word by breaking it down into parts that you recognize, such as the root word, a prefix, or a suffix. This vocabulary strategy is called **structural analysis.**

Another vocabulary strategy is using **context clues**, or hints from the text surrounding the unknown word.

When all else fails, a dictionary or glossary can give you a word's definition.

On the next page you will find examples of how vocabulary strategies can help you figure out the meanings of unfamiliar words.

Biology is formed from two Greek roots. Bio means "life" and logy means "study of."

The sentence tells you that depict has something to do with describing dolphins. The same Latin root, pict, is in the word picture.

The words entertained, audiences, and tales should tell you what bards are.

Regaled is defined by the appositive following it.

Two Latin roots combine in transformed. Trans means "over." Form is "shape."

Myths depict dolphins differently than do the cold descriptions of biology. Ancient Greek bards regaled, or entertained, their audiences with tales of these sea creatures. They said that the god Apollo transformed himself into a dolphin, seized a ship, and steered it to land. He persuaded the passengers to become priests in his temple. The Greeks also believed that pirates once captured the god Dionysus. The pirates thought that he was a human instead of a deity. Dionysus changed his captors into dolphins. The Greeks said the reason dolphins are friendly to humans is that they were once mortals themselves.

The words instead of show that deity is an antonym, or opposite, of human.

Capt, the Latin root for "seize," is the base of captor. The suffix -or means "one who."

This sentence suggests that humans is a synonym for mortals.

Listening and Speaking Strategies

Listening is an important skill that takes practice.

Listening well doesn't come naturally for many people. Here are some strategies to improve your listening skills.

Identify Purpose

Just as you set a purpose for reading to help you read better, you should also set a purpose for listening. Decide what you are listening for. Three general purposes for listening are **listening for information**, **listening for direction**, and **listening for appreciation.**

Think About Your Behavior

- Listen to others as you would like them to listen to you.

- Keep your mind open to other people's feelings and ideas.

- Show respect by giving your attention to the speaker.

- Don't interrupt.

- Respond appropriately. That can mean clapping after a performance in a theater, or asking questions after your classmate gives an oral report.

Speaking effectively is one of the most important skills you'll ever learn.

Speaking is our main way of communicating our ideas, opinions, and feelings to other people. To become a confident and effective speaker, you should **identify your purpose**, **prepare**, and **practice**.

Identify Purpose

Think about your purpose for speaking. Decide what you want to say and why you think it's important. The four general purposes for speaking are **sharing information**, **giving directions**, **entertaining**, and **persuading**.

Prepare

Prepare your speech well ahead of time by researching your subject and making notes. Study your notes so that you are thoroughly familiar with your subject.

Practice

You can practice giving your speech by yourself or with a partner. Speak clearly, slowly, and loudly enough to be understood. Refer to your notes when necessary.

Perfect!

Researching Information

> "Knowledge is of two kinds. We know a subject ourselves, or we know where we can find information upon it."
>
> Samuel Johnson (1709 – 1784)

Research is not just something you need to do for school. Think of research as a helpful learning tool that you can use for many different purposes. You can go to a library and use your research skills to find magazine and newspaper articles as well as books about topics that interest you. **Skimming, scanning,** and **taking notes** are useful skills that will help you do research more effectively.

- **SKIMMING** means looking over a book or reference source quickly to identify its subject and find out how it is organized. Divisions and headings will help you locate sections that you want to go back to and read carefully.

- **SCANNING** means looking quickly through a passage to find key words or phrases. Scanning is a fast way to locate specific information.

STUDY SKILLS

- **TAKING NOTES** is a good way to summarize your research. You can take notes in a notebook or on index cards, depending on what method you find easier. Here is an example of notes taken from an encyclopedia article:

Write the topic at the top.

Write only what you need to remember.

Use your own words.

Use short phrases instead of sentences.

Write the name of the source.

Dolphins
small, toothed whales
mammals (not fish):
lungs, warm-blooded,
constant body temp.
intelligent
highly developed hearing,
vision, touch
no-sense of smell
little or no sense of taste
World Book Encyclopedia, 1991

Notes can be useful when you give a speech or write a report, so use your own words and include only what you think you want or need.

STUDY SKILLS

Libraries contain books, periodicals (such as magazines and newspapers), reference materials (such as atlases, encyclopedias, and almanacs), government documents, and audiovisual materials. Libraries are organized into areas such as **fiction**, **nonfiction**, **periodicals**, and **reference sources.**

Nonfiction

You can locate **nonfiction** books by using the **card catalog**. Each book is listed on three different cards: by **title**, by **author**, and by **subject**. Cards are filed in alphabetical order in drawers.

The subject card lists the subject of the book first.

The author card lists the author's last name first.

The title card lists the title of the book first.

599.5   DOLPHINS

599.5   Patent, Dorothy Hinshaw
        Dolphins and Porpoises/Dorothy

        Dolphins and Porpoises
599.5   Patent, Dorothy Hinshaw
        Dolphins and Porpoises/
            Dorothy Hinshaw Patent
        New York: Holiday House. ©1987

Many libraries now use **computerized catalogs**. Like card catalogs, computerized catalogs are organized by title, author, and subject.

000 — 099 **General works**
(encyclopedias, atlases, newspapers)

100 — 199 **Philosophy**
(ideas about the meaning of life)

200 — 299 **Religion**
(world religions, myths)

300 — 399 **Social Science**
(government, law, business, education)

400 — 499 **Language**
(dictionaries, grammar books)

500 — 599 **Pure Science**
(mathematics, chemistry, plants, animals)

600 — 699 **Applied Science**
(how-to books, engineering, radio)

700 — 799 **Arts and Recreation**
(music, art, sports, hobbies)

800 — 899 **Literature**
(poems, plays, essays)

900 — 999 **History**
(travel, geography, biography)

(Note: Many libraries separate biographies from the 900s and organize them in alphabetical order by the subject's last name.)

Each nonfiction book has a call number that is listed on its three cards (or on the computer screen) and on the book itself. The library shelves are labeled with the call numbers of the books they contain. Call numbers based on the Dewey Decimal System are used to arrange nonfiction books by subject area. (See chart.)

Fiction

Books of fiction do not have call numbers. They are organized in alphabetical order by the author's last name. They are listed in the card catalog just as nonfiction books are.

Periodicals

You can locate information in a magazine or newspaper by using the *Reader's Guide to Periodical Literature.* Many libraries also store information about periodicals in computers.

Reference Sources

Libraries have many references, including specialized dictionaries, atlases, indexes, and maps.

Note: Italic page numbers refer to additional practice.

A

Abbreviations, 177, *236–237*
Additional practice, *179–237*
Addresses, 92–93
Adjectives, 27, 138–145, *202–205*
Adverbs, 27, 160–163, *220–222*
Agreement of subject and verb, 170
Apostrophe, 128–129, 132, *196–197*
Appositive, 173, *231*
Articles, 138–139, *202*
Audience for writing, 14, 38

B

Brainstorming for writing ideas, 15

C

Capitalization, 124–125, 176, 177, *234–235*
Clause, 116–117, *190–191*
    dependent, 118–119, *191*
    independent, 118–119, *191*
Combining sentences, 26
Commas, 114–115, 172–175, *230–231*
    after introductory words and
      phrases, 172, *230*
    in compound sentences, 114
    in direct address, 172, *230*
    series, 173, *231*
    with appositives, 173, *231*
    with interrupters, 173, *231*
Comparisons
    using figurative language, 28
    with adjectives, 142–145, *204–205*
    with adverbs, 162–163, *222*
Computers, using, 25
Conclusion, writing a, 23, 65
Conferences, revising, 24
Conjunction
    coordinating, 114–115, *188–189*
    subordinating, 118–119, *190–191*
Contractions, 132
Creative writing, 40–53
Cross-curriculum writing, 69, 74–77

D

Descriptive writing, 54–55
    See Writing forms and models.
Details
    adding, 27
    sensory, 56, 58–59
    supporting, 75, 76–77, 81, 102
Dialogue, 174–175, *232–233*
Direct object, 150–151, *210–211*
Direct quotations, 174–175, *232–233*
Drafting, 12, 22–23, 41, 55, 61, 79, 87, 99

E

Edited draft, 29
Editor's marks, 26, 30
Envelope, 93
Everyday writing, 86–87
    See Writing forms and models.
Exact words, 28
Examples, adding, 27
Expanding sentences, 26
Expository writing, 60–77, 84–85

F

Figurative language, 28
Final draft, 33

G

Grammar, 103–167
Graphic organizers, 16–21
Group writing, 34

H

Handwriting chart, 178

I

Indirect object, 150–151, *210–211*
Interjection, 107
Interview, conducting an, 70
Introduction, writing an, 23, 58, 65

J

Journal, 15, 88, 89

L

Letters. *See* Writing forms and models.
Library, the, 252–253
Listening. *See* Speaking and listening.

M

Math, writing for, 69
Mechanics, 172–177, *230–237*
    See also Commas, Quotation marks, and Titles.
Metaphor, 28
Multicultural perspectives, 111, 122, 127, 137, 161

N

Narrative writing, 40–53
    See Writing forms and models.
Narrowing a topic, 16–17
Negatives, 163, *223*
Note taking, 37, 96
Nouns, 123–129
    common, 124–125, *194*
    plural, 126, *195*
    possessive, 128–129, *196–197*
    proper, 124–125, *194*
    singular, 126, *195*

O

Object of the preposition, 164–165, *224–225*
Opinion, 78–85
Outline, 21, 72

P

Period, 106, 108, 177
Phrase, 116–117, *190*
    adjective, 166, *226*
    adverb, 167, *227*
    prepositional, 27,165, *225*
Portfolio, for writing ideas, 15
Predicate, 109–110, 112–113, *184–187*
    complete, 109, *184–185*
    compound, 112–113, *186–187*
    simple, 110, *184–185*
Predicate adjective, 152–153, *212–213*
Predicate nominative, 152–153, *212–213*
Preposition, 164–165, *224–225*

Prewriting, 12, 14–21, 40, 54, 60, 78, 86, 98
Pronouns, 130–137, *198–201*
    antecedent, 134–135, *199*
    object, 132, *198–199*
    possessive, 136, *200–201*
    reflexive, 133, *198–199*
    subject, 132, *198–199*
Proofread draft, 31
Proofreading, 13, 30–31, 41, 55, 61, 79, 87, 99
Publishing, 13, 33, 41, 55, 61, 79, 87, 99
Purpose for writing, 14, 40–41, 54–55, 60–61, 78–79, 86–87, 98–99

Q

Quotation marks, 174–175, 176, *232–233, 234–235*

R

Research Report, 74–77

Revising, 24–29

S

Science, writing for, 69
Sentences, 104–105, *180–181*
    capitalization in, 104
    combining, 26
    complex, 120–121, *192–193*
    compound, 114–115, *188–189*
    declarative, 106, *180–181*
    detail 27, 56–58, 62
    editing wordy, 28
    exclamatory, 107, *181*
    expanding, 26
    imperative, 108, *181*
    interrogative, 106, *180–181*
    simple, 114–115, *188–189*
    topic, 56–57, 64, 66–69

Simile, 28
Speaking and listening
    interview, 70
    message, 91
    play, 52–53

publishing ideas, 32–33
revising conferences, 24
speech or oral report, 84–85
Spelling, 30, 31
Story. *See* **Writing forms and models.**
Study skills, 239–253
Subject, 109–113, *182–183*, *186–187*
complete, 109, *182–183*
compound, 112–113, *186–187*
simple, 110, *182–183*
verb agreement, 170

T

TAP, 14
Task, 14
Test, writing for a, 98–102
Thesaurus, 25
Thesis statement, 79, 80, 85, 101, 102
Time order, 43, 58, 62, 66, 73, 76–77
Titles, 176, *234–235*
Topic
choosing a, 40, 54, 60, 78, 86, 98
narrowing a, 16–17
sentence, 56, 57, 64, 66, 67–69, 100

U

Usage
common errors, 170–171
troublesome words, 168–169,
228–229

V

Verbs
action, 146–147, 152–153, *206–207, 213*
future tense, 154–155, *214–215*
helping, 148–149, *208–209*
intransitive, 150–151, *210–211*
irregular, 158–159, *218–219*
linking, 146–147, 152–153, *206–207*
main, 148–149, *208–209*
past tense, 154–155, *214–215*
perfect tenses, 156–157, *216–217*
present tense, 154–155, *214–215*
principal parts of, 158–159, *218–219*
subject-verb agreement, 170
transitive, 150–151, *210–211*

Viewing, 52–53, 83
Visuals, 84–85
Vivid words, using, 28

W

Wordy sentences, editing, 28
Writer's notebook, 90
Writing for a test, 98–102
Writing forms and models
book review, 82
cause and effect, 68
character sketch, 57
comparison and contrast, 67
descriptive essay, 58–59
descriptive paragraph, 56
directions, 66
folktale, 46–47
forms, 94–95
information article, 65
information paragraph, 64
journal, 15, 88, 89
letter
business, 93
envelope, 93
friendly, 92
messages, 91
movie review, 83
myth, 48–49
news story, 70–71
note taking, 96
personal narrative, 62–63
persuasive essay, 80
persuasive letter, 81
play, 52–53
poems, 51
research report
biography, 73
science, 74–75
social studies, 76–77
speech/oral report, 84–85
story
historical fiction, 44–45
realistic fiction, 42–43
summary, 97
tall tale, 50
Writing process, 12–13
Writing to learn, 36–37